CHAI
the spice tea of india

diana rosen

STOREY
BOOKS

The mission of Storey Communications is to serve our customers by publishing practical information that encourages personal independence in harmony with the environment.

Edited by Deborah Balmuth and Robin Catalano
Cover design and illustration by Carol Jessop, Black Trout Design
Cover photograph by Giles Prett
Interior design and production by Jen Rork
Production assistance by Erin Lincourt
Photographs by Giles Prett except:
pages 5, 6, 12, 14, 16, 17–19, 63–66, 73, 74, 84, and 119 by Dinodia Picture Agency;
pages 11, 39, and 67 by John Conte; page 25 by Thomas P. McHugh; and page 120 by Deborah E. Burns
Indexed by Peggy Holloway, Holloway Indexing Services

Printed in Canada by Transcontinental Printing

10 9 8 7 6 5 4 3 2 1

**Library of Congress
Cataloging-in-Publication Data**

Rosen, Diana.
    Chai : the spice tea of India / Diana Rosen.
       p.   cm.
    Includes bibliographical references.
    ISBN 1-58017-166-4 (pbk. : alk. paper)
    1. Tea—India.   I. Title.
TX817.T3R67   1999
641.6'372—dc21   99-18361
                                   CIP

contents

dedication

To *chaiwallahs* everywhere.

acknowledgments

No book is ever a solitary effort, and this one is no exception. Many thanks to Frances Wood of the Oriental and India Office Collections, the British Library, London, England; to staff librarians at the San Francisco main library, and research librarians at the Corte Madera and Sausalito public libraries, for assistance above and beyond the call of duty. To tea industry professionals Michael Harney, Harney & Sons; Anupa Mueller, Eco-Prima, Inc.; Frank Miller, Blue Willow Tea Company; Mike Olsen, Time for Tea; Devan Shah, India Tea Importers; and Manish Shah, My Chai, many thanks for insight into India and its magnificent tea industry.

India is a friendly Tower of Babel, and many natives know several languages or dialects. For their expertise and translations, my thanks to Sarra Baraily, Laurel Bunce-Polarek, Anupa Mueller, Devan Shah, Manish Shah, and their families, who offered advice in Bengali, Urdu, Hindi, Sanskrit, and several other Indian languages, plus terms created by the British influence on India over the years. Those words that have a variety of sources but are used by everyone I have dubbed "Indian," although there is no such language. There are words, particularly those related to food and chai spices, that are understood by everyone in India, regardless of their mother tongue.

Many thanks to Chef Robert Wemischner for his luxurious recipes; to personal chef Carolyn Manzi, and to baking enthusiast and teacher Gary Stotsky, for their fun twists on chai treats and desserts; and to Sally Champe for her chai recipe.

To chai enthusiasts Gary and Jan Routh and their home page, http://www.sni.net/chai, chai lovers and chai blenders, thank you for your input.

To friends and supporters Joe and Patti Anastasi, Suzanne J. Brown, Diana Payette, Dona Schweiger, Amy Ulmer, and so many more, thanks for the encouragement!

To the superb staff at Storey Books and Storey Communications and to editors Deborah Balmuth and Robin Catalano, many thanks (again!); and thank you to designer Jen Rork for shaping pages of words into an artful book.

Chai ka maza
lele, tumhara
din khil
jaayaga.

(Take the enjoyment
of chai — your day
will blosom.)

— TRADITIONAL
INDIAN SAYING

special thanks

Thanks to the following for sharing their recollections: Sarra Baraily for "A Tea Lover Finds Her Ultimate Cup"; Karen Benke for "My First Cup of Masala Chai"; Michael Harney, Harney & Sons, Salisbury, Connecticut for "A Tea Blender Visits Assam"; Frank Miller, Blue Willow Tea Company, Seattle, Washington, for "Garam Chai, Chai Garam"; Mike Olsen, Time for Tea in Philadelphia, Pennsylvania, for "A Tea Shop Owner Visits Darjeeling"; and Terre Pasero, Larkspur, California, for "A Tourist Visits the Taj Mahal."

Grateful acknowledgment is made to the following writers who contributed poems: Ranjit Hoskote, assistant editor, *The Times of India*, Mumbai, Bombay, first prize winner in the IndiaStar All-India Poetry Competition, 1997; Sudeep Sen, writer and literary editor, New Delhi, commendation prize winner in the IndiaStar All-India Poetry Competition, 1997, based on Henri Matisse's painting *Femme à l'amphora*, 1953; Shampa Sinha, a writer currently studying law and economics at the University of Tasmania, Australia, and winner of the first prize in the All-India Poetry Competition, 1993, organized by the Poetry Society (India); and for "The Taj Mahal," Rabindranath Tagore. Unless otherwise attributed within the text, all interviews, stories, and tales are the work of the author.

the journey begins

When tea was served in these special chai cups,
it also took on that very special,
wonderful other taste of the earth.

— MADHUR JAFFREY,
AUTHOR OF NUMEROUS COOKBOOKS
AND AN AUTHORITY ON INDIAN CUISINE

Sounds, smells, heat, dust.

These are currency in the memory bank of everyone who has ever visited the complex, fascinating country called India. While some visitors seek a spiritual connection, others absorb the majesty of the scenery, from the towering Himalayas to the genteel luxury of the Goa seaside or the countless other exotic sights that lure thousands of tourists here every year.

For lovers of the leaf, like me, the lush green tea gardens are a must-see. The first stop for many of us is Darjeeling, home of the "champagne" of teas; next, Nilgiri, where we can inhale the fragrance of the Blue Mountains. Certainly we must travel to the birthplace of the Indian tea industry, Assam, with the fabled Brahmaputra River cutting through the greatest tea-growing region of this incredible country.

India's richly layered culture attracts travelers to its Hindu temples, built thousands of years before Christ was born, and a reminder that Hinduism is alive and well and practiced by millions. Buddhist temples abound, a testament to more than thirteen centuries of presence in India. There are Muslim temples, Jewish synagogues, and churches and temples for many other religions, concrete examples of applied tolerance.

Other man-made wonders, like the Taj Mahal, lure visitors to the more romantic side of India. This monument from a shah to his beloved wife is more than a tomb, it is a work of art from the vibrant Moghul period (A.D. 1526–1738), when Islam was the religion of the ruling class.

Today India is the world's largest democracy, despite turbulent times and constant changes, chaotic weather including yearly monsoon rains, mountains so high they literally take your breath away, and a vibrant patchwork quilt of culture found nowhere else on earth. Since opening its doors to foreign investors in the last few decades, after years of economic isolation, India has experienced tremendous progress, and some growing pains. As in centuries past, part of India's wealth lies in its incredible range of spices that have lured adventurers to this country and continue to fascinate chefs and diners alike.

These condiments inspired world trade and not a little piracy. They continue to intrigue, although today it is businesspeople who come through the traditional channels of commerce for spices that not only give sparkle to complex cuisines, but provide health and cosmetic benefits. Perhaps the most significantly "new" role for Indian spices is scenting and flavoring the Indian spice tea specialty called masala chai.

Tea people connect with tea in the way a monk connects with his monastery — when he is in his monastery he is in a state of total bliss.

— JULIE SAHNI, AUTHOR OF *JULIE SAHNI'S INTRODUCTION TO INDIAN COOKING*

A Traveler's Tale

My First Taste of Indian Masala Chai

As the train pulled into the station, the noise level rose. Turbaned young men climbed onto the sides of the trains, each balancing a tray with grace and skill with one hand while gripping the steel handles of the train with strength and perseverance with his other.

The aroma of the beverage they offered was amazing. It filled me up, welcomed me, got my full attention. Looking around, I sensed the rhythm of this tea dance of climbing tea sellers who shouted what became a two-syllable campaign to sell "Chai-ee, chai-ee." Passengers signaled the tea servers with hands outstretched from train windows holding a few rupees. With staccato movements, the sellers managed to serve all of us, moving down the line of each car quickly, efficiently, and smoothly before jumping down from the final car onto the station walkway to await the next train, rolling in behind us.

What I received for my few rupees was an unglazed little cup full of a thick, milky drink. It was hot, spicy, nurturing, calming. Clattering sounds grabbed my attention away from the reverie I was having with my Indian spice tea. The clitter-clatter was the result of the little cups, hundreds of them, being tossed from the train windows to crash onto the train tracks below.

As an American and a Californian, I admit that my first reaction was, "How wasteful." Then a smiling gentleman next to me assured me this was the custom. Tentatively, I dropped my cup from my window and watched it splatter when it hit the ground with a faint *plop* just seconds before the train picked up speed and headed out to our next stop.

The smiling gentleman turned out to be traveling to my own destination, and proceeded to tell me the story of masala chai.

"Those servers," he said, "they are *chaiwallahs*, tea sellers, whose days begin before dawn and end after dusk. This is how they make their living. Some even make their own cups; others buy them from people whose only work is making these cups." Leaning forward slightly, he said quietly, "It is hygienic to drink from disposable vessels like these."

Sitting back in his seat, he continued with his story of a day in the life of a *chaiwallah*. "Each has his own recipe," he said. "They use ground black tea, not the whole leaves or good-quality broken leaves that only the wealthier Indians can afford. No, they brew this ground black tea with their own combination of spices: pepper, cardamom, cinnamon, maybe cloves or ginger." He counted them off on his fingers.

The most familiar sight to train travelers in India: the welcoming cup of chai, poured carefully during the brief station stops.

Pepper, I thought, pepper? Yes, I realized, that was part of what warmed me and made me feel so good when I sipped this new-to-me drink.

"The *chaiwallahs* boil this brew several times," the gentleman added. Seeing my reaction, he laughed. "It is not your fine Darjeeling, not Margaret's Hope or Castleton, but it is what we call, how you say? — *maza*, great fun.

"The mixture is boiled several times with milk," he repeated, "then strained and served to customers. It is kept hot by pouring it into an urn or a metal teapot, just like those you saw *chaiwallahs* use to pour the tea into the little clay cups. Clever, yes? Tomorrow he will do it again, and the next day."

Built in 1799, the Hava Mahal, or Palace of the Winds, is one of the most famous landmarks in Jaipur.

During my travels I thought about the gentleman's remarks many times, as I sampled masala chai at every train stop. I soon came to adore its unique and comforting taste. The tea was just as wonderful on street corners where capitalism, with all its accompanying competition, marketing, and selling styles, came alive with what I call "the dance of the *chaiwallahs*."

Because most *chaiwallahs* were selling the same brew from most likely the same main source, the only way they could ensure a sale was to add flamboyance and not a little chutzpah to draw customers to their respective street corners. With each cry of "chai-ee," a *wallah* would hoist his teapot as high as his eyes and pour the tea into little clay cups with great finesse, superb hand-eye control, and perhaps a bit of luck. Those who spilled even a drop were laughed at or, worse, lost a sale. I would often buy more than I actually wanted just to see this acrobatic display of showmanship.

Times have changed for the *chaiwallahs,* as tourists have discovered during trips to India. Nowadays one is more likely to be served chai in Styrofoam cups, or to receive chai made not with milk but who-knows-what. Still, visitors all come to treasure those first fabulous cups of masala chai on introductory trips to the land of spices, India, and try whenever possible to duplicate this pleasure at home.

what is chai?

In India, where its people speak many many languages, the generic word for tea is chai. It derives from the Chinese word for tea, *cha*, which the British turned into *tay*, which then evolved into *tea*; this is what the western world came to call the leaf of the *Camellia sinensis* plant. Today, both the Japanese and the Chinese say "cha" for tea, and the Indians say "chai."

The focal point of this book, however, is the tea drink known as masala chai. This beverage reflects the addition of masala, a combination of several spices that are popular in various Indian cuisines. Here in America, many masala chai blenders offer premade drinks with milk and call them chai lattes, following the style of the popular milky coffee drinks.

Whether it's called by the "proper" name of masala chai, or the generic name, chai, this stimulating, calming, nourishing drink of tea, spices, and sometimes milk and sugar is utterly delicious.

Choosing and Brewing Indian Teas

Indian teas grow in three regions — Darjeeling, Assam, and Nilgiri — and each region produces fine blacks, some oolongs, and some greens. The blacks of each area are great in chais and offer different flavor profiles for your chai. Darjeeling, for example, is lighter and more delicate and goes well with cardamom. Nilgiri teas accept flavorings easily and will not cloud when iced. Assams are great for hot chais and can hold up well with stronger spices like pepper and ginger. Experiment with all three to see what tastes best to you.

To brew with loose leaves, measure out one teaspoon. Add about six ounces of hot water (195–200°F) to the leaves and allow to steep for several minutes, or as suggested by your tea merchant or tea blender. Strain and serve.

No matter which chai recipe you use, warm up your mug or cup first by filling it with hot water. Let it sit for about a minute, discard the water, and you'll have a nicely warmed receptacle for your favorite chai.

Siesta

After lunch
when the flies had stopped buzzing
over the food-littered floor
and the air
was still and heavy
when only the soft plop
of drops from a leaky tap
into a half-filled tin pail
broke the quiet
my wrinkled grandmother
would ask me to comb
her long wet hair
and as the comb furrowed
through the dark shining mass
and the smell of her coconut hair oil
mingled with the warmth of
midday sunshine
her lips would tell me
of how an illiterate peasant
had obtained the gift of rhymes
from the Goddess Saraswati
of how the new-born Krishna
had escaped the wrath of
a jealous king
and of many other
such bygone things
I would look on
with sleep-drunk eyes
as she recited Sanskrit verse
in a grating sandpapery voice
and when
her eyes closed in comfort
and her breathing became as rhythmic
as the poetry she had chanted
through the long lazy afternoon,
I would tiptoe
up to the old wall clock
to see if time had stopped.

— Shampa Sinha

Making Indian Tea into Masala Chai

To make your Indian tea into chai, add spices to the loose tea leaves, then add the water. Allow the water to boil with the leaf/spice mixture for about five minutes or more. Add milk and simmer for another five minutes. Strain and serve.

An alternate way of brewing chai is to strain the leaf/spice mixture and add heated milk prior to serving. Or you can add sweetener at the same time you add the spices to intensify the sweetening ingredient. Some people prefer to add the sweetener upon serving. If it's the richness of fine tea flavor you want, avoid oversteeping. For CTC black tea (sometimes called ground tea) cooking it with spices and milk for a long time only enhances all of the flavors.

The Magic of Tea

I have gathered a collection of favorite recipes, anecdotes and travelers' tales gleaned by charmed visitors to India, who share here the pleasures they receive from the remarkable drink called chai.

I will give a glimpse at the unique history of tea in India; we'll take side trips to the country's three major tea-growing regions and I will introduce some classic and contemporary Indian poetry, share thoughtful observations on this wildly diverse country, and give you a great time.

Please join me on the road to discovering the pleasures of masala chai and the fine teas of India.

the history of indian tea

Tea is much more than a mere drink. . .
It is a solace, a mystique, an art,
a way of life, almost a religion.
— Cecil Porter,
Gemini News Service

China has grown and used tea as a beverage for thousands of years, yet India's earliest recognition of the tea plant dates from only the first century A.D., and no records of India's wild tea plant being made into a beverage exist at all. Yet in less than two centuries (since the early 1800s) India has become the largest producer of tea in the world. Drinking tea there now is almost akin to breathing.

The story of the modern tea industry in India is inextricably bound up with the story of British presence there. It begins as the Empire was aided, abetted, and assisted by the most powerful commercial venture of the world at that time, the East India Company.

the persistence of the EIC

The East India Company was founded in 1600 as "The Governor and Merchants of London Trading into the East Indies," under the royal charter of Queen Elizabeth I, to trade with the spice islands of the East Indies (Indonesia). The company subsequently introduced its spices to the West Indies and many other stops around the globe.

Pursuing trade routes to the Orient, it was instrumental in creating two of the most powerful port cities of trade, Singapore and Hong Kong. This enabled the company to grow so large that it had all the strength and power of a country: its own army and navy, its own currency, and its own territories.

In the seventeenth century, the EIC introduced China tea to Great Britain. The matchmaking worked: Britain remained the EIC's chief Chinese-tea customer for nearly two centuries. Indeed, the Empire's purchases of tea began to adversely affect its budget. The company tried to balance this assault on British coffers by selling British goods to China, but the Chinese continually refused to buy them. Emperor Ch'ien-lung, who ruled from 1736 to 1796, reportedly informed King George II that "I set no value on strange or ingenious objects and have no use for your country's manufactures." What he did have use for was silver bullion. This was the only British item the emperor would accept for his tea, and for his other popular selling commodity, silk.

Trade Wars

It was the EIC, not King George, that was actually responsible for the infamous Boston Tea Party in the United States. Anxious to settle its growing pile of debts and whittle down an expanding stock of tea, the company "encouraged" the British government to pass the Tea Act of 1773, which allowed it to sell tea to the Americas, collect taxes on tea,

While tea has been cultivated in China for centuries, it wasn't until the mid-nineteenth century that India joined the tea-growing industry.

and open up a new port of trade. Neither the EIC nor the royal court realized how the colonists would react to such high taxes. The captains of EIC ships were met with protests at Boston, Charleston, Philadelphia, New York, and Annapolis before the company finally realized the error of its ways. (Americans continued to buy chintzes from the EIC but refused tea well into the nineteenth century.)

Incidentally, the EIC also began transporting Bengal-grown opium from Calcutta to China as part of its attempts to balance international trade. This was in direct violation of an imperial prohibition on opium smoking in China and the Edict of Peking, which forbade import of the drug. For a while it was believed that this infamous attempt at the balance of trade between two world powers would be helpful, but it depleted the coffers of both countries in order to feed two addictions (although tea can certainly be deemed harmless compared to opium). It was not until 1906, nearly seven decades after the violent first Opium War (1839–1842), that China and Great Britain finally agreed to a reduction of opium growing in India.

The British Crown finally absorbed what remained of the East India Company in 1874, ending a remarkable chapter of history in which a commercial firm was able to hold world leaders prisoner (Napoleon), hire pirates to do dirty deeds (the most famous of these was Captain Kidd), and help Elihu Yale establish one of the greatest personal fortunes in America — which continues to support the university that bears his name.

queen victoria steps in

The success of the EIC was due in no small part to the support of Her Majesty Queen Victoria (1819–1901). The queen, whose beverage of choice was Scotch, was keenly aware of her subjects' thirst for tea. She also understood that her country's continually wavering financial position was as much at the mercy of China's appetite for silver during her reign as it had been for nearly a century before her. Eager to keep her inherited silver at Windsor, so to speak, she realized that growing tea "at home" in India would be infinitely easier than continuing the trade wars with the Chinese. She requested, as only royals can, that everything be done to grow tea in one of her colonies.

The East India Company was only too willing to help, but it was four particular Britons who literally did the

The top two leaves and bud of the *Camellia sinensis* bush make the finest tasting tea.

work. This quartet of pioneers included two Scottish brothers, C. A. (Charles Alexander) and Major Robert Bruce; Lord William Charles Cavendish Bentinck; and the English botanist Robert Fortune.

Cutting a Path through Assam

The Bruce brothers had been stationed for a number of years in India, then Great Britain's largest colony. They were happy to heed their queen's request. Major Robert Bruce explored what was then known as Burmese Assam in 1823, where he made several botanical forays into the nearby Beesa Hills. There he "discovered" native tea trees. (An Indian native, Moneram Dewan, actually pointed out the

a tea puzzle

Robert Bruce's "discovery" of wild tea plants in Assam leads to a conundrum: Did those plants originate in India, or did they come from China? If they in fact originated in India, why was there no tea drinking there until the British arrived? The beverages historically drunk in India were made from herbs.

Geography provides a clue to help solve this riddle: The region of Assam lies near India's eastern border with China, and many Buddhist monks made the trek to and from China and India. One such Chinese monk, Gan Lu, who lived during the Han Dynasty (A.D. 25–221), recorded his travels to India to study Buddhism. When he returned to China he brought back the seeds from a new-to-him plant, the tea bush. Buddhist monks in Korea, Japan, India, and China followed his example and each soon discovered that tea was just the brew to stimulate devotees to remain steadfast in their hours of prayer and meditation. All began planting tea seeds on their respective monastery properties. This does not, however, mean that tea was unknown elsewhere; China, Viet Nam, and Nepal have tea bushes dating back hundreds of years. The riddle continues.

plants to the major.) In 1825 his brother C. A. took some seeds from those Assam tea bushes and, as an experiment, planted them in his own garden in Sadiya, a town in Darjeeling. Major Robert Bruce died that same year, before he could know that his simple "discovery" of a wild Assam tea plant would found an entire industry.

The year 1825 is important in the birth of the India tea industry for yet another reason. The English Society of Arts offered a gold medal or fifty guineas "to the person who shall grow and prepare the greatest quantity of tea of good quality, not being less than 20 pounds in weight, in the East or West Indies, or any other British colony." Although Lieutenant Andrew Charlton received this gold medal, historians usually attribute most of the work during this pioneering era to C. A. Bruce.

The rolling hills of India make a stunning backdrop for this tea plantation.

the first commercial assam tea

A former lieutenant in the Royal Navy, C. A. Bruce was the first Superintendent of Tea Culture, although he was not educated in botany. He was, however, an experienced explorer who had lived in India many years and understood its climate and people, particularly those of Assam.

Barely accessible and barely livable because of enormous floods from heavy monsoons, Assam was thoroughly dangerous as a breeding ground for malaria-carrying mosquitoes. Undaunted, C. A. spent more than four years cutting a swath through the Assam forests, planting and cultivating tea plants. These efforts finally paid off when, using the simplest of techniques, he made the first drinkable Assam tea for the British market. His methods involved withering the tea leaves in the sun, rolling them by hand, and drying them over charcoal fires. Thankfully for historians of tea, he recorded his findings shortly thereafter in a pamphlet called *Account of the manufacture of the black tea as now practiced at Suddeya, in upper Assam, by Chinamen sent thither for that purpose, with some observations on the culture of the plant in China, and its growth in Assam.*

Other British planters soon took up Bruce's work in Assam. After traveling by boat up the Brahmaputra River, often for as long as a month at a time, they entered the jungle on elephant, lived in makeshift huts, and helped clear the bug-infested jungle. Their companions were solitude, wild animals, and the ever-present danger of cholera, yellow fever, dysentery, and malaria. Many died, but those who survived were able to send for their families, build better housing, and establish a community that reflected their cultural roots: polo, cricket, and Sunday outings "at the club." Of course, these Englishmen did not perform this backbreaking work alone, but literally enslaved many local Indians, giving rise to the phrase that Assam was "bitter tea," a sentiment barely eased by growing Indian independence in the twentieth century.

Interest in the infant India tea industry was growing, but Chinese teas still lured both vendors and consumers. This grew particularly worrisome in 1833, when Britain's trade treaty with China expired and the Chinese government chose not to renew it. On January 24, 1834, Governor General Lord William Charles Cavendish Bentinck (1774–1839) therefore convened the now-famous Tea Committee, charging it to submit a plan for introducing Chinese-tea culture into India. He gave great attention to his task, gathering the data, organizing it, and drawing conclusions. Alas, he died before his work could be completed. Many tea pioneers and historians feel that Great Britain owes Lord Bentinck a debt of gratitude for bringing Chinese tea plants to India.

wild tea is found in nilgiri

In the early nineteenth century, *Camellia sinensis* var. *assamica* plants were discovered throughout the Nilgiri Hills — just as they had been in Assam and, later, Darjeeling. This was a surprise to many British tea pioneers, who believed these hills, lower in altitude than Darjeeling, would not be hospitable to tea growing. Instead, Nilgiri's milder overall climate and constant moisture proved to grow luxuriant tea bushes.

Because the wild tea plant was found in so many places, it was assumed that everywhere this plant grew would be hospitable to easy cultivation. But this was not the case: Swamps had to be drained, land cleared, and tea bushes planted. These labor-intensive jobs took months, even years to accomplish. It was not until 1953 that commercial tea planting truly began in Nilgiri.

The committee continued Bentinck's work, successfully introducing the first lot of Chinese tea seeds throughout India: in Assam, the Himalayas of Darjeeling, and the Nilgiri Hills.

Britain Annexes Assam

The year 1838 was momentous in the history of tea in India: Great Britain "annexed" Assam, enabling it to control and develop this vital tea-growing region. The first eight chests of commercial Indian tea were shipped to London in December 1838, and sold at India House in January 1839 with the East India Company serving as the primary vendor. As it turned out, the quality of the tea left much to be desired. Still, this 1839 auction proved a great promotional effort for the new "British-grown" tea.

The Asiatic Journal furnished this rather breathless account of the first sale of Assam tea in London:

Everywhere you travel throughout India you'll find street vendors serving their piping hot chai to tourists and natives alike.

"The first importation of tea from the British territories in Assam, consisting of eight chests, containing about 350 pounds, was put up by the East India Company to public sale in the commercial sale rooms of the tea and commodities market, Mincing Lane, on 10th January, 1839, and excited much curiosity. The lots were eight, three of Assam souchong, and five of Assam pekoe. On offering the first lot (souchong) Mr. Thompson, the sale-broker announced that each lot would be sold, without the least reservation, to the highest bidder. The first bid was 5s. per pound, a second bid was made of 10s. per pound. After much competition it was knocked down for 21s. per pound, the purchaser being Capt. Pidding. The second lot of souchong was bought for the same person for 20s. per pound. The third and last lot of souchong sold for 16s. per pound, Capt. Pidding being the buyer. The first lot of Assam pekoe sold after much competition for

24s. per pound, every broker appearing to bid for it. It was bought for Capt. Pidding. The second, third and fourth lots of Assam pekoe fetched the respective prices of 25s., 27s., 6d., and 28s., 6d. per pound and were purchased for Capt. Pidding. For the last lot (pekoe) a most exciting competition took place, — there were nearly 60 bids made for it. It was at last knocked down at the extraordinary price of 34s. per pound, Capt. Pidding was the purchaser of this lot, and has therefore become the sole proprietor of the first importation of Assam tea. This gentleman, we understand, has been induced to give this enormous price for an article that may be produced at 1s. per pound but the public-spirited motive of securing a fair trial to this valuable product of British Assam."

fortune smiles on the empire

The story of the British cultivation of tea in India is one of trial and error, travail and trespassing, and utter tenacity. The tale continues now with the man who most successfully brought healthy Chinese plants to India: English botanist Robert Fortune, Botanical Collector to the Horticultural Society of London.

World-renowned in his own lifetime, Fortune was responsible for bringing countless trees, flowers, and vegetables to both Great Britain and India. His acute professionalism and thorough agricultural education enabled him to cut, preserve, and keep alive precious tea bush cuttings in ways that helped them live throughout the arduous trip from Canton to Calcutta.

Fortune set out for China in the fall of 1842 to collect cuttings of various plants and seedlings. But Fortune was — like all pioneers — an

Taking cuttings from tea bushes is considered "women's work" in India, and the tea pluckers are highly skilled and supremely efficient.

adventurous soul not given to defeat and eager to achieve his goals at any cost. In a chatty writing style, he recounted his adventures in enormous detail in several popular books of the time.

An Englishman to the core, Fortune was at first totally unfamiliar with any tea other than what he had enjoyed in London — black tea served with sugar and milk. His first reaction to drinking tea in China was not unlike that of many Western tourists, both then and now. He did, however, show great openness to new taste adventures, to wit:

"The good lady of the house set down a teacup before each of us, into which she put some tea, and then filled each cup up with boiling water. I need scarcely say she did not offer us any sugar or milk. . . . We drank our tea, which I found most refreshing, in its pure state without sugar and milk. Now and then someone connected with the house came round and filled our basins again with boiling water. This is usually repeated two or three times, or until all the strength is drawn out of the leaves."

The Work Continues

Through both charm and perseverance, Fortune made the acquaintance of many helpful guides. He traveled to tea plantations throughout China, sometimes on foot and other times by sedan chair, a common contraption of the time carried by four Chinese men. On several occasions he dressed to appear Chinese — which must have been quite a feat, though he insisted that he did indeed "pass."

At every stop along the way, it was Fortune the botanist at work, preparing cuttings, seedlings, and young tea bushes to send from Canton to Hong Kong to Calcutta. After many delays, he wrote, "In October and November [of 1849] I procured a large supply of tea-seeds and young plants from Hwuy-chow, and from various parts of the province of Chekiang. These were all brought to Shanghae in order to be prepared and packed for the long voyage to India. When they were all gathered together into Mr. Beale's garden they formed a collection of great interest. Here were tea-plants, not only from Silver Island, Chusan, and the districts about Ning-po, but from the far-famed countries of Sung-lo-Shan and the Woo-e hills. A number of the cases were now ready for the reception of the plants, and the whole of them were taken down to Hong-kong under my own care. They were then divided and sent on to Calcutta by four different vessels, in case of accident.

"During the summer of 1850," Fortune continued, "I had the satisfaction of hearing that my collections of tea-plants had arrived safely at Calcutta. . . . One of the objects of my mission to China had been, to a certain extent, accomplished. The Himalayan tea-plantations could now boast of having a number of plants from the best tea-districts of China, namely, from the green-tea country of Hwuy-chow, and from the black-tea country of the Woo-e hills.

"Since my return to Shanghae I had been engaged in getting the tea-plants carefully planted in Ward's cases, in order to send them to India. As there was no vessel in Shanghae bound for Calcutta direct, I determined to take the collection to Hong-kong, and to ship them thence to India."

The Ward's cases that Fortune mentioned (they were named for their designer, N. B. Ward) were made of mahogany or oak and featured glass tops, not unlike old curio cabinets. They were glazed to be nearly airtight so that moisture would not creep in and destroy the plants. (Glazing was the only effective technique in that era before plastic wrap and aluminum foil.)

On February 16, 1851, Fortune left Shanghai on the *Lady Mary Wood* with sixteen glazed Ward's cases filled with various plants and tea seeds. He arrived in Calcutta on March 15. "The mulberry-plants were found to be in good condition, and the tea-seeds had germinated during the voyage, and were now covering the surface of the soil," he wrote. By this simple plan about twelve thousand plants were added to the Himalayan plantations in Darjeeling.

With this gargantuan effort, the Indian tea industry finally had all the resources and tools it needed to really establish itself. In less than a decade — on December 27, 1861 — the first regular tea sale was held in Calcutta of tea from leaves grown in India. This sale was followed by another on February 19, 1862. To further speed distribution, a railway line was built in the 1880s to get the tea from plantation to auction sooner and safer, which did much to strengthen the industry. Today auctions are generally held in Calcutta every week during the seasons.

indian tea in the twentieth century

Great Britain gained enormous wealth during its years of tea trade in India, and hundreds of fine tea blenders made fortunes creating signature blends. Following India's independence from the United Kingdom on August 15, 1947, some tea estates were transferred to local management, although British-owned companies still have a strong presence in the country.

There is no small irony in the story of India's tea industry. Although it began as a way to use one of Britain's territories to prevent the Empire's wealth from leaving its shores for China, today's Indian tea industry supports a viable and independent democracy that no longer labors under any queen.

classic masala chai

He boils milk with . . . tea that is so dark and fine-leaved that it looks like black dust. He strains it and puts cane sugar in both our cups. There's something euphorically invigorating and yet filling about it. It tastes the way I imagine the Far East must taste.

— PETER HØEG, *Smilla's Sense of Snow*

for years I have enjoyed and written about the fine green and white teas of China, the crisp blacks of Sri Lanka, the sophisticated greens of Japan; all have been delectable and many quite memorable. Yet I always go back to the teas I first tasted during childhood — Darjeeling, Assam, and Nilgiri, the tea triumvirate of India. The difference between what I drank as a child and my adult choices is the difference between a beverage made with more milk than tea, plus a big spoon of sugar, compared with estate-caliber teas steeped briefly and carefully and drunk plain, savored as much for their spiritual components as for their seductive taste.

The single-estate teas of my adult experience — Darjeeling Goomtees or Nilgiri Tiger Hills — are of paramount importance to many tea lovers, but still relatively unknown. Instead, what has captured the public's attention so vividly these days is masala chai, a casual tea beverage made with buffalo milk, loaded with exotic spices, and drunk primarily throughout northern India. This drink is as common there as Coca-Cola is here in the United States. (Coffee is drunk in southern India, along with a spice tea, but it is not the milky chai of the north.)

Masala chai is not a serious drink; it's fun. It's full of the unexpected taste sensations of fiery and sweet, soft and harsh. For all its contradictions, it is calming and delicious to enjoy by itself, with desserts, with a meal, or, as the Indians do, with spicy savories. The savories, in fact, represent an entire chapter in the huge "book" of Indian cuisines, and I offer many examples of the most classic of these dishes.

A TRAVELER'S TALE

"Garam Chai, Chai Garam"

During the 1960s I was a volunteer in the Peace Corps, and my first home was in the center of a magnificent tea garden in the state of Punjab in northwestern India. This was not just a blind date with tea, it was a chance encounter. Up to this time I had never been a tea drinker, and I certainly had no inkling that twenty-five years later I would own my own tea company.

The Bandla Tea Estate was planted among the gently rolling hills just outside the town of Palampur, 5,000 feet high in the foothills of the Himalayas. The gardens were lush with dark green tea bushes pruned flat to waist height, elegant shade trees, and a labyrinth of tiny gurgling irrigation channels. Passing through the tea garden to and from the bazaar, I observed daily work rhythms, seasonal changes; people, flora, and fauna seemed to thrive there. Even someone unaware of tea and its traditions would have loved this place for its enchanting beauty and serenity, and I was no exception.

Not all of Peace Corps life was quiet and unassuming, though. In the mid-1960s, India and Pakistan engaged in the first of what would be two wars over shared borders; the battle zone was barely 100 miles from our tea garden. The U.S. Embassy was adamant that we abandon our station, but four of us wanted to hold our ground. When Ambassador Chester Bowles sent his big black Chevy Carryall to evacuate us, we knew we had better move down to New Delhi.

I had little to do there other than socialize with other Americans displaced by the war, so I mapped out a rail tour of India that took in the major sights of northern India and parts of the south. Following this

FRANK MILLER, owner and tea buyer of Blue Willow Tea Company in Seattle, Washington, has had a long romance with tea that first blossomed during his sojourn in India nearly thirty years ago. Miller's own "secret formula" is part of the allure of his version of this Indian nectar, appropriately called Seattle Chai.

itinerary, I would trace the major tea-growing regions of India: Darjeeling and Assam in the north and the Nilgiris, or "blue mountains," in the south.

All Peace Corps volunteers traveled third class, a result of both an unspoken rule and economic imperative. Today this would not be such an insurmountable hardship; during the 1960s, however, third-class rail travel was like traveling with the entire rural population of India . . .

Tea and travel go hand-in-hand in Indian culture.

all in a single car. There were no seats as such, just hard wooden benches without upholstery or forgiveness.

Ventilation was provided by two tiny oscillating fans covered with oil-soaked dust. Coal soot flurried in through open windows to smear itself on clothing and exposed skin. Families carried what appeared to be all of their worldly possessions. Infants and toddlers were undiapered; people ate highly spiced foods that filled the rail cars with their aromas; sometimes live animals, tied by the feet, stood between family members and other passengers. The cacophony of many languages added noise to what was, in truth, uncompromising discomfort. Nevertheless, we four youths crisscrossed the subcontinent in a relatively carefree manner, taking in some of the most unusual sights in the world, and because of our age (this *was* thirty years ago!) and natural enthusiasm, we loved it.

At night sleep was fitful; the click-clack of the train would lull us into semiconsciousness, then the wailing air brakes and squealing wheels stopping at a station would jar us awake. In the twilight zone between short snoozes and bleary consciousness, usually at an unreasonable 3 A.M., came the plaintive cries of the red-turbaned *chaiwallah,* "Chai garam, garam chai," "hot tea, hot tea," slowly getting louder as we whooshed into the station. In southern India he would be wearing a *dhoti,* a traditional white cloth wrapped around the waist; in the north he wore billowy white pajamas covered by an untucked, oversized shirt. The costume, however, was beside the point; the main event was the noisy activity on the railway platform, a signal for us to count our Indian paise in preparation for his quick visit. Suddenly, this implausibly energetic man would career toward our open window, push a creakily built wooden cart toward us, and offer the elixir of life, hot chai.

This thick, orangy drink was a simmered milk tea made of half fresh buffalo milk, half Nilgiri broken or CTC tea leaves, plus lots of sugar. Each thick white ceramic cup or tiny unfired clay bowl was filled to the brim with this molten hot, treacly brew — hotter than you could hold without scalding yourself, which you did, and which woke you up proper. This is what I call "station chai," a treat as ubiquitous and as welcoming as the "station noodles" of Japan.

In many large Indian cities it is not uncommon to see people and animals walking side-by-side with cars, trucks, and even rickshaws pulled by men.

Since then I have tried hundreds, actually thousands, of teas of every hue and style, from the most expensive Darjeeling FTGFOP I (clonal) to the rarest China tribute tea, but nothing compares with the vibrant lifesaving cups of chai that came sloshing out of the *chai-wallah*'s carbon black teakettle. Drinking that chai in the noisy, crowded train station in the middle of the night, in the middle of nowhere, was part of what even today makes India and tea seem so mystical and so wildly exciting.

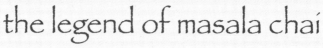

the legend of masala chai

How did this fascinating spice tea develop in India? One legend, certainly apocryphal, avers that the chef for a royal king of India created this tea by scenting it with the luxurious fragrance of spices from his kitchen: cloves, nutmeg, and cardamom.

The king, entranced by the unique taste of his chef's special tea, announced that this drink could be served only in his court and forbade the chef to divulge its ingredients. Long after the king's death, however, the recipe filtered down from royalty to the aristocracy and then to the masses, with each group adding and deleting spices to its tastes, including cinnamon, pepper, fennel, and more.

Tibetans, who have used tea as a sacred offering and beverage of hospitality since the tenth century, boiled their tea with salt and goat's milk and later with salt and yak butter. Tibetan monks traveling to India and bringing the combination of milk and tea to that country are another possible source of masala chai recipes.

No matter where it began, though, it's clear that the spice tea of India can intrigue anyone, in any era or station of life.

masala chai in india

The typical style of tea preparation throughout southern India is English, complete with porcelain teapot and cups, sugar and milk, but no spices. This is not to say that Indians outside of the north do not drink spice tea. When they do, however, they use perhaps one cardamom pod per pot of beautifully made, whole-leaf tea of exquisite aroma and taste, plus milk and sugar. This is a very simple recipe compared to most chais made here in the United States or the spicy northern Indian masala chais.

What is it about the spicy chais of India's north that have captivated me — and so many other tea lovers? Is it the exotic combinations of spices that warm us all over? Is it the sweetness of sugar and richness of whole milk that comforts? Or is it a drink that simply tastes wonderful?

The Tea

Masala chai (spice tea) is generally made with black teas, although many commercial manufacturers have begun preparing

British pots, cups, and saucers are the teaware of choice in India.

classic chai recipes with green teas, combinations of black and green teas, or herbal infusions, to great success. As always, the better the quality of tea, the better the final product will taste. Any of the following, or a blend of two or three, will do: Indian Assam, Nilgiri, or Darjeeling; China Keemun; Uva, Dimbulla, or Ceylon blacks from Sri Lanka. Typically, masala chais for the Indian masses are made from inexpensive "ground tea" — black tea ground nearly to a powder — or rough low-grade black teas processed by a method known as CTC (crush, tear, curl). These are cheap, providing many cups to the pound, and have a heavy, intense taste that stands up well to spices and milk.

The Spices

India was and remains one of the premier sources of exotic spices. The sophistication and complexity of Indian spices are so vast, in fact, that I can only touch on the subject here. (There's more information about spices on pages 88–102, although even that treatment hardly does the subject justice.) Every region — from Bengal to Punjab, from Assam to Kashmir, from Bombay to New Delhi, and everywhere in between — has had chefs who favored one spice or spice combination over another, creating cuisines specific to each local region.

Tea — unless one is drinking it in the Russian style — should be drunk *without sugar*. . . .

How can you call yourself a true tealover if you destroy the flavour of your tea by putting sugar in it? . . .

If you sweeten it, you are no longer tasting the tea, you are merely tasting the sugar. . . .

Try drinking tea without sugar for, say, a fortnight and it is very unlikely that you will ever want to ruin your tea by sweetening it again.

— GEORGE ORWELL,
"A NICE CUP OF TEA"

The exotic cuisines of India, from north to south, have for centuries each used the spices native to its own area: the pungent peppers and chilis, the sweet bite of ginger, cinnamon, or cloves, the softness of cardamom, the pleasures of aniseed and its close cousin fennel seed, along with lemongrass, vanilla, allspice, coriander, and so many more. Just as spices differ in cuisine from region to region, so they differ in spice teas.

Not all masala teas have the same spices, but cardamom, cinnamon, cloves, and black pepper are generally used in northern India. Other recipes may include cumin or coriander. The variety and proportions of spices also vary with each chef.

The Sweetener

Sugar. Orwell's criticism about sugar aside, both Great Britain and India love sugar with their tea, and both countries owe their love of this sweetener to the spice traders of the fifteenth century — particularly Christopher Columbus, who introduced sugarcane to the West Indies.

A tropical plant, sugar continues to grow in the West Indies and in South and North America, particularly Hawaii. It grows to enormous heights (20 feet) and produces a bamboolike cane.

While sugarcane has been around for nearly five centuries, sugar beets have only been used popularly since the late 1800s. A field crop grown throughout the plains of North America, the sugar beet has fat, parsniplike roots from which the sweet beet sugar is extracted.

Molasses sugar, a dark unrefined sugar with a high quantity of molasses, is fantastic in masala chais, because its dark richness is a perfect balance to the spiciness of fresh ginger or pepper. Another excellent sweetener is raw Barbados cane sugar, also known as jaggery (*goodh*). Jaggery is the preferred sugar for sweets in all the provinces of India. It is an unrefined sugar made by boiling the juice of sugarcane or palm sap to thicken it, pouring it into molds, and allowing it to dry into a lumpy mass. Turbinado sugar and Demerara sugar from Guyana are both excellent brown sugars in chais.

Honey. Domestic beekeeping dates to the Bronze Age and before, and honey is the preeminent sweetener, and preservative, around the world. Much of honey's flavor relies on its flower source, from lavender to clover, from orange blossom to herb flowers like thyme and rosemary. Orange and clover honeys are ideal for chais because they add a delicacy that can, nonetheless, stand up to the other more pungent spices used in the mélange. Colors can range from nearly clear to thick yellow or opaque cream, but each has a hint of golden color.

The Milk

Generally, rich whole milk is used in Indian cooking, and chais are no exception. Some chai lovers enjoy their brew with condensed milk or unsweetened evaporated milk, and the lactose-intolerant opt for soy, oat, or rice milk, with excellent results. For the richest taste, do not use a nonfat product.

Flavored honey is the preferred tea sweetener for many people.

The Finishing Touches

Chais come in many colors, and you can use these to create some dramatic presentations. You might serve your chai in Russian-style tea

buffalo milk?

Buffalo milk has sometimes been used for Indian chais. However, the best-quality, richest whole cow's milk is a more typical choice. If you must use low-fat or nonfat milk, heat until it is reduced somewhat to give it that thick, creamy taste. Condensed milk is also good.

preparing chai for a crowd

Making chai in quantity is fairly straightforward. Tea bags are ideal: Just toss one tea bag per person, plus two or three more (to taste), into a pot, then add 6 ounces of water per person. As always, though, loose-leaf teas give a better flavor; use at least 1 teaspoon per person, and a heaping one for the pot.

When the tea has fully brewed, add one serving or 6 ounces of milk to the pot. Another alternative is to brew the tea bags in milk, rather than water, for a more intense, creamier flavor. Do not boil the milk.

It's always a good idea to use fresh whole spices, rather than ground ones, when making chai, because ground spice flavors tend to fade. So slice that fresh ginger, shred that cinnamon stick, and crush those peppercorns. Your crowd will ask for more.

glasses with metal holders, or in Irish whiskey glasses. Mugs or cups with intense colors of rust or terra-cotta, red, green, or even the basic blacks or whites can all mirror the color of your chais.

Just as you might add a stick of cinnamon, a dusting of cocoa, a quick grating of nutmeg, or a sprinkle of sugar to a coffee drink, you can do the same with your chais. And don't forget the whipped cream! Who said a chai shouldn't be as decadent as it is delicious?

the basics of masala chai

Preparing chai from scratch at home is easy and provides a brew with more complex layers of flavors. The basic ingredients include tea, at least four spices, water, and milk. The spices are commonly cinnamon, cardamom, ginger, and cloves, but pepper, allspice, and fennel (or aniseed or star anise), are also excellent. Some chai lovers like to brew the tea first, toss in the spices at the last minute, then add warmed milk. I prefer to put the tea and spices into cold water, heat it to boiling, and then continue to cook at a simmer for three to seven more minutes. I believe that adding the spices in this manner provides a more pungent taste that is as good for your palate as it is for the spices.

Equipment for Making Chai at Home

Brewing chai is as simple and easy as brewing tea. It's even easier if you opt for soluble powdered mixes. (I'll discuss these more fully in the next chapter.) All you need then are a kettle (to heat the water), a measuring cup (to measure the milk and water), and a cup or mug (to pour the chai into before its pungent sweetness warms you up).

To brew chais with liquid concentrates, tea bags, or loose-leaf teas, all you need is a saucepan and a strainer. Add water and/or milk to the concentrate (or tea bags or teas), plus more spices as necessary, warm it up, strain, and serve.

classic masala chai

masala
spice mixture

The blend at right is a good basic spice mixture for chais. As always, let your own taste preferences guide you, adding or deleting spices and adjusting quantities as you like.

Mix all ingredients thoroughly. Store in a tightly lidded glass jar in a cool, dark place.

¹/₄ cup

2 tablespoons ground
  cardamom

2 tablespoons ground
  cloves

2 tablespoons ground
  cinnamon

2 tablespoons powdered
  ginger

1 tablespoon ground
  black pepper

masala tea

Whole milk works best in this chai, but unsweetened condensed milk is a good alternative. One heaping teaspoon of tea per serving is perfect. If you are using tea bags, one per person will do, but for stronger tastes make this with two tea bags per person.

1. In a saucepan, bring the water, sugar, and tea leaves to a boil.
2. Add the Masala Spice Mixture and bring to a second boil.
3. Add the milk and simmer about 5 minutes.
4. Preheat cups (see page 7). Strain the chai, pour it into the warmed cups, and serve immediately.

2 servings

½ cup water

2 teaspoons sugar

2 teaspoons Assam or
  Darjeeling tea
  leaves

⅛ teaspoon Masala
  Spice Mixture
  (see above)

½ cup milk

sally champe's masala chai

1 14-ounce can unsweet-
ened condensed milk
(low-fat or nonfat, if
desired)

½ teaspoon ground
cardamom

¼ teaspoon ground
allspice

¼ teaspoon ground
cinnamon

¼ teaspoon ground
cloves

⅛ teaspoon ground
black pepper

My friend Sally Champe, a veteran traveler who has lived in India, has the simplest at-home chai recipe I've ever tried, and it makes a perfect beverage every time. She keeps a can of spice-infused unsweetened condensed milk in the refrigerator; it is at the ready whenever the craving for chai surfaces. She just puts on a tape of Indian music, relaxes, and savors the taste of India.

1. Pour the entire can of milk into a clean, dry jar.
2. Add all the spices and cover tightly with a lid.
3. Place in the refrigerator. The longer it stays refrigerated, the better it gets.
4. To use, stir the mixture, and scoop out 2 to 3 tablespoons directly into a cup of very strong, very hot black tea. Ah!

1¾ cups

diana's
favorite chai

Experimenting with quantities and varieties of spices has been intriguing (and delicious). Although I admit to continually "adjusting," this is now my current favorite mixture.

1. Put the water and spices into a saucepan and bring to a boil.
2. Reduce the heat to low and let simmer for about 6 minutes.
3. Add the milk and sugar and heat to almost boiling.
4. Add the tea and turn off the heat. Allow the brew to infuse the tea for 3 minutes.
5. Prewarm two teacups (see page 7). Strain the chai brew and serve.

2 servings

1½ cups water

8 green cardamom pods

6 whole black peppercorns

2 slices fresh ginger, peeled and diced

1 stick cinnamon, 2 inches long

2 whole cloves

⅔ cup whole milk

4 teaspoons sugar

3 teaspoons loose black Assam tea

Chai for two can be a relaxing, intimate experience.

4 cups water

1 cinnamon stick

1 1-inch piece of ginger, peeled and cut into 4 slices

12 green cardamom pods

8 allspice berries

8 whole cloves

1 teaspoon coriander seeds

4 teaspoons black tea leaves

1 cup milk

Honey to taste

adriana's
chai

In their New York shop and book, Adriana's Spice Caravan *(see Recommended Reading) Adriana and Rochelle Zabarkes provide a lot of insight into cooking with rubs, marinades, and blends created with spices grown around the world. This is their recipe for classic chai.*

1. Combine the water and spices in a saucepan over medium heat and bring to a boil.

2. Reduce the heat to low, cover, and simmer for 20 minutes.

3. Add the tea and milk and simmer over low heat for 3 more minutes.

4. Sweeten with honey, strain through a fine sieve, and pour into prewarmed cups (see page 7) immediately.

4 servings

Nilgiri is a fine black tea to use in chai recipes.

classic masala chai

masala chai
concentrate

Making your own concentrate can save time and money. It can be refrigerated for more than a week; just reheat with water or more milk for your own fresh-tasting hot chai (see page 36 for instructions).

1. Crush all the spices and mix them together. Pour the milk into a medium saucepan, and then add spices and sugar.

2. Heat over medium heat until bubbles start to form.

3. Stir frequently at a low simmer until the liquid is reduced by half (about 45 minutes).

4. Remove from the heat and pour through a fine sieve or cheesecloth.

5. The concentrate will last longer if it's chilled down quickly. If you do not intend to have a cup of chai immediately, take the warm milk mixture and place it in a bowl of ice cubes. When the liquid is cool, or at least lukewarm, it can be refrigerated.

*2 cups concentrate
(enough for 14 to 16 servings)*

20 **cardamom pods**

20 **whole cloves**

20 **black peppercorns**

2 **3-inch sticks of cinnamon**

5 **allspice berries**

1 **½-inch or larger slice of fresh ginger, peeled and crushed**

4 **cups whole milk**

1 **teaspoon sugar**

how to use concentrate

When you're ready for a cup of chai, assemble the ingredients and follow these steps.

1 teaspoon black Assam or Nilgiri leaves steeped in 1¼ cups boiling water for 3 to 4 minutes

2 tablespoons chai concentrate, heated with 1 table-spoon whole milk

1 teaspoon sugar or honey, or to taste

1. Pour the brewed tea into a cup.
2. Add the heated milk-and-concentrate mixture.
3. Add sugar or honey to taste. Drink up!

1 serving

masala chai
comes to america

**If the stranger say unto thee
that he thirsteth, give him a cup of tea.**

— CONFUCIUS

In the last few years masala chais have taken the United States by storm. Every day there is a new brand to try, new versions in tea and coffee shops to sip, new ways to cook with masala chai — or chai latte, as the beverage has come to be called.

Masala chais are now, I am happy to note, a fixture on the menus of the most sophisticated of coffee bars, in restaurants, and even on the grocer's shelf. Those who have already discovered masala chai have been as calmed and nourished by this drink as I. Abdicators from the "Camp of Coffee" have recognized that all the fun of coffee drinks is inherent in chai lattes, too: foamy beards of milk, a bite from the spices that replaces the buzz of coffee's caffeine, and the sweetness of honey or sugar.

Perhaps, unlike the soothing nightcap of warmed milk or hot chocolate of our youth, masala chai's spices make it an infinitely more sophisticated and adult drink. Certainly it is interesting, even surprising for the innocent palate.

As always, American manufacturers have added invention to convention. Today's choices cover every dietary requirement or restriction you can imagine: unsweetened, low-fat, decaffeinated, lactose-free. Or consider chai made not with tea but herbs for an entirely new beverage with the classic spiciness of traditional chais. Whether it's because of our heritage of a strong dairy industry or our nation's predilection for sweets, chai lattes created by U.S. firms and those made in shops and restaurants are much sweeter and creamier than the Indian classic ever is.

For convenience, try ready-to-drink bottles and aseptic boxes, tea bags, and liquid concentrates for large groups or for cooking. Some powdered mixes only require adding hot water; some brands enclose a scoop to make sure you put in just the right amount of mix to liquid. Both concentrates and powders tend to be sweeter and milkier than chais made from scratch, but there is no argument that they are mighty easy and neat to prepare. And if you have a cappuccino machine at home, the milk steamer is an ideal tool for heating milk for your chai, making the tea frothy and milky at the same time. (See recipe on page 41.)

Reading the ingredients list on American chais is frequently an eye opener, though. The milk may not be a dried milk powder; in fact, it may not be milk at all, but a nondairy creamer. In addition to sugar and/or honey, there may be corn syrup, sucrose, and other sweeteners. Most prepared chai mixes do not contain full-leaf or even broken-leaf teas, but either tea powders or concentrates made from tea.

Fortunately for lovers of the leaf, there are also masala chais that emphasize the tea — excellent choices of spice-infused loose-leaf tea that you can brew up yourself, adding sweetener and/or milk to your individual taste. You needn't forsake a taste for fine tea to enjoy masala chai. Many companies have developed a variety of chais made with high-quality black tea or fine green tea and lots of tasty, freshly ground spices.

Spice-tea blends that contain only tea and ground spices enable you to add the milk of your choice: soy, rice, oat, or cow's milk. You can also mix in the sweetener of your choice in the amount that suits your palate, like brown or white sugar or honey.

Whether you create your own spice blends, use prepared blends, or buy a preblended tea, the basic spices used in most loose-leaf spice teas are cardamom, cinnamon, ginger, and cloves. Most chai lovers agree that this beverage cries out for experimentation, so follow your instincts about quantities and adding other spices like pepper, allspice, fennel, or your personal spice favorites.

KAREN BENKE is a writer who teaches in the California Poets in the Schools program, which brings the magic of poetry to children in all grade levels. Ms. Benke's own poetry and short fiction have been published in several literary journals and anthologies. She is completing her first novel.

My First Cup of Masala Chai

Autumn finds me in class, with another cold. I am standing at the chalkboard in Jacquie Faber's third-grade classroom, coughing.

As a teacher in the California Poets in the School program, I introduce poetry to eager children. Today I ask my eight-year-old students to put metaphors into their poems. "Instead of saying something's very good or really hot or as lovely as lovely can be," I sniffle, "give me a picture of what's good, hot, and lovely."

Students show me the November sky and their grandmother's herb garden, and the mountain where they found their first favorite rock. Listening, Ms. Faber hands me a warm mug of something steamy she has just prepared, saying, "Have some chai?" She smiles one of her blessed smiles, then sits down to write her own poem.

Looking out the tall windows at the maple trees, I breathe in cinnamon, love, and kindness.

chais for special diets

Anyone can enjoy a masala chai these days no matter what the food allergy, dietary restriction, or taste preference. The objective is to make a hot (or iced) drink that excites the palate, calms the nerves, and pleases the stomach.

Milk-Free and Low-Fat

So you like the frothy taste of chai but you're lactose-intolerant? The answer is easy: Use either oat, soy, or rice milk. Best of all, the quantity of milk used for both lactose and nonlactose drinks is the same; if the recipe calls for ¼ cup of milk, then ¼ cup of oat, soy, or rice milk will do. You can also use fat-free oat, soy, or rice milk, although you will not create as rich tasting a drink. Increase the spices and/or the sugars to compensate for the lack of richness due to the reduced fat content in the milk.

Sugar-Free Chai

Who doesn't love sweets? Still, if you're counting calories, or if you're a diabetic, you won't even miss chai's sweetener if you amp up its spices or use whole or unsweetened condensed milk. The spices will add a complex flavor profile, and the condensed milk will create a frothy rich taste that will more than compensate for sweetening. Using saccharin, aspartame, or other sugar substitutes does *not* work well with chai because these artificial sweeteners leave a decidedly bitter aftertaste. Add a pear juice or apple juice concentrate if traditional sweeteners are not for you.

chai "cappuccino"

Your favorite chai recipe can take on the consistency of a cappuccino if you add steamed milk. Prepare the chai brew as usual then, at the same time, pour the tea and the warmed milk into the cup. If you have an espresso machine with a milk steamer, using it will greatly enhance the texture and flavor of the hot milk in your drink. Serve in a heavy white porcelain cup and saucer, add a sprinkle more of cinnamon or cocoa, and you have a chai "cappuccino."

Decaf Chai

There are two points of view regarding decaffeinated chais: Use a decaf black tea as a base, or use an herbal brew as a base. My personal choice is to use rooibos, from the African red bush, or to use red clover, a common herbal tea available everywhere herbal infusions are sold. Each takes well to the masala spices.

If decaf black tea is your choice, opt for a decaf breakfast blend, decaf Assam, or decaf Keemun. The natural heartiness of these teas will give you that tea "bite" without the caffeine, and stand up well to the masala spices. An alternative choice is a decaf Nilgiri.

chai recipes with a twist

Now that you know how to make traditional and popular chais, it's time to uncork the imagination and transfer the taste of masala chai to other foods and drinks. I hope these inspire you!

chai milk shake

Here's a fun twist on masala chai. Simply brew your favorite black tea chai recipe and let it cool, then strain out the tea and spices. Add two scoops of vanilla, ginger, or mocha ice cream to a blender jar, pour in the chai, and blend until frothy. (If you want to be adventurous, add fresh fruit like strawberries, cantaloupes, or bananas for a creamy frappe.) Pour into a chilled tumbler and serve with a long spoon and straw. Yum!

carolina chai cocoa

Personal chef Carolyn Manzi added a little punch to packaged powdered chai mix and came up with this universal winner. This is very sweet and chocolaty.

1. Stir together the chai mix and cocoa powder.
2. Add the hot water and stir thoroughly.
3. Prewarm two thick mugs (see page 7), pour in the Chai Cocoa, add a dollop of whipped cream to each mug, and dust with more cocoa on top. Serve immediately.

2 servings

3 tablespoons powdered chai mix

3 tablespoons fine unsweetened cocoa powder (Italian or Dutch)

2 cups hot water

Whipped cream

What could possibly be better than a cup of hot, frothy chai? Chai with rich, velvety chocolate, of course!

chai toddy

2 tea bags of chai
spice-and-tea mix

1½ cups water

1 jigger dark rum

1 jigger apple brandy

2 tablespoons (¼ stick)
unsalted butter

12 small brown sugar
cubes

On cold, damp, wintry days on Cape Cod, this chai recipe really hits the spot. It was created by personal chef Carolyn Manzi.

1. Put the tea bags and water in a saucepan and heat until boiling. Continue boiling at least 2 more minutes.
2. Add the rum, brandy, butter, and sugar. Stir over low heat until the sugar dissolves. Pour into two clear, prewarmed mugs (see page 7). Serve immediately.

2 servings

The typical chai spices blend perfectly with liqueur in this variation on the traditional hot toddy.

kashmiri chai

Just as there are hundreds of masala chai recipes, Kashmiri chais vary, but all use light spices and are boiled for hours. This recipe is considerably less intense than most, yet it has both strength and delicacy in the perfume of the cardamom and almonds.

1. In a small saucepan, boil the water with the cardamom pods. Infuse for about 10 minutes. Add the tea and crushed almonds and infuse to taste, about 4 minutes.
2. Strain and serve with hot milk and sugar, as desired, in thick, heavy prewarmed mugs that keep this comforting drink hot.

4 servings

6¾ cups water

12 whole crushed green cardamom pods

4 teaspoons ground black tea

1 tablespoon crushed raw, unsalted almonds, the consistency of coarse meal

green kashmiri chai

This simple-to-make version of chai is made with green tea, preferably a gunpowder or perhaps a Darjeeling or Assam green.

Boil the water, then add the tea leaves and sugar and let steep for 2 or 3 minutes. Add the spices and almonds and remove from the heat. Serve immediately in preheated clear cups or mugs. (See page 7).

4 servings

4 cups water

1½ teaspoons green tea

2 teaspoons sugar, or more to taste

2 teaspoons ground green cardamom

Pinch of ground cinnamon (⅛ teaspoon)

6 grated almonds

green tea chai

**12 whole crushed green
cardamom pods**

6¾ cups boiling water

**3 tablespoons green
Assam or Darjeeling
tea leaves**

**1 teaspoon ground
cinnamon or
2 cinnamon sticks,
shredded**

**1 teaspoon ground
cloves**

While some green tea chai stalwarts feel that any green tea will do, I prefer the more complex greens of India, like Assam or Darjeeling, which stand up to the spices better. Chinese and Japanese green teas are sweeter and lighter in taste and should preferably be drunk plain. If you prefer Chinese or Japanese tea, using cardamom only is a lovely, and less overwhelming, addition. If you prefer more spices in the green tea, this recipe calls for ground spices, which tend not to overwhelm green teas the way the more biting whole spices can.

Put the cardamom pods in the boiling water and infuse for about 10 minutes. Add the green tea and infuse for another 2 minutes. Add the cinnamon and cloves. Strain and serve. This looks particularly lovely served in dark green or celadon cups to make the brew look even greener.

4 servings

herbal
spice chai

This is great anytime, but especially when you have a cold and do not want to use regular tea. Of course, you could always add the shot of whiskey that most cold toddies call for, but that's truly optional. Rooibos (African red bush) is available at most herb and tea shops.

Steep the rooibos in the water for about 6 minutes. Add the spices and honey. Strain and serve immediately. Because the rooibos is reddish, opt for a rust- or red-hued mug, or a clear cup to show off the color.

2 servings

2–3 tablespoons rooibos (African red bush)

1½ cups boiling water

1 teaspoon lemongrass

½ teaspoon ground cinnamon (or 1 shredded stick)

1 tablespoon honey

mocha chai

Who doesn't like chocolate? Here's a way to elevate a chai latte to chocoholic heaven.

2 tablespoons loose-leaf Assam tea

1½ cups boiling water

½ cup whole milk or ¼ cup unsweetened condensed milk

½ teaspoon ground cinnamon

¼ teaspoon ground cloves

1 tablespoon cocoa

Whipped cream (optional)

Cocoa for dusting (optional)

1. Steep the tea in the water for about 5 minutes. Add the milk, spices, and cocoa and simmer over low heat about 2 or 3 minutes more.

2. Prewarm two mugs (see page 7). Pour in your mocha chai, add a dollop of whipped cream and a dusting of cocoa, if you like, and enjoy. Serve immediately.

2 servings

You'll want to use the biggest mug you can find to savor a delicious mocha chai.

iced chai

Any of your favorite chai recipes can be iced. For best results, the tea should be brewed slightly stronger than usual so that the ice will not water down the taste.

Allow the brewed tea to cool slightly, then pour it over ice. For a slushy consistency, pour the chai and ice cubes into a blender and blend for about 30 seconds or as needed. Serve in a chilled tumbler or, for a slush, in a chilled parfait glass for an elegant touch.

1 serving

1 cup prepared chai

Ice cubes

baking with chai

The inherent spiciness of chais make them ideal for perking up baked goods. When using cardamom, opt for white for appearance or pale green for best flavor.

- ½ cup dry chai mix
- 1 pound Neufchâtel or cream cheese
- ¼ cup sugar
- 2 large eggs
- 1 teaspoon pure vanilla extract
- 1 ready-made 8" graham cracker piecrust
- ¾ cup whole fruit jam (such as strawberry or blueberry)

chai cheesecake

1. Preheat the oven to 375°F.
2. Cream together in a bowl the chai mix, cheese, sugar, eggs, and vanilla. Pour into the crust and level with a rubber spatula. Bake for 20 minutes.
3. Remove from the oven and cool. Refrigerate for 2 hours. Garnish with fruit jam, cut into wedges, and serve.

12 discreet pieces or
6 hefty servings

tea masala cake

This scrumptious cake was developed by enthusiastic amateur baker Gary Stotsky, whose many creative recipes for afternoon tea entertaining have graced the pages of TEA TALK, A Newsletter on the Pleasures of Tea *for a number of years.*

1. Preheat the oven to 350°F.
2. In a bowl, beat together the margarine, sugar, vanilla, and egg. Stir in the chopped apples.
3. In a second bowl, sift all the dry ingredients together. Add the dry ingredients to the moist, and mix thoroughly into a dough.
4. Turn the dough into a greased 8-inch square pan, and bake for 45 minutes.
5. Cool in the pan for 12 minutes, then turn the cake out onto a rack to cool completely.

9 large servings

¼ cup (½ stick) margarine or butter

1 cup sugar

1 teaspoon vanilla extract

1 large egg

2 cups well-chopped apples

2 teaspoons Masala Spice Mixture (see page 31)

1 cup all-purpose flour

½ teaspoon baking powder

chai scones

SCONES

- 3¾ cups (1 pound) all-purpose flour
- ½ cup well-packed dark brown sugar
- 1 teaspoon baking powder
- 1 teaspoon ground cinnamon
- 1 teaspoon ground cardamom
- 1 teaspoon ground ginger
- ½ cup (1 stick) unsalted butter
- 2 large egg yolks
- ¾ cup heavy cream or half-and-half
- ⅔ cup masala chai concentrate

The rich, warm spiciness of masala chai finds its way into these buttery scones created by Chef Robert Wemischner, a pioneer in cooking with tea. The dough can be made in advance if it's well wrapped and frozen at 0°F. It will keep in the freezer for up to a month.

These taste best warm and dotted with jam, Devonshire cream, or softly whipped sweetened cream. The recipe can be halved or doubled as desired.

The scones include a premade masala chai concentrate. The spices have been "amped up," and the dough is topped with a sprinkling of cinnamon and sugar just before baking. For a lower-fat version, make these with milk instead of cream or half-and-half.

1. Preheat the oven to 425°F.
2. To make the scones, sift together all the dry ingredients into the bowl of an electric mixer. Add the butter. Mix on low until the mixture resembles coarse meal.
3. In a small bowl, combine egg yolks, heavy cream or half-and-half, and masala chai concentrate. Add the moist mixture to the dry ingredients and mix by hand just until combined; do not overmix or scones will be tough.
4. On a lightly floured surface, knead the dough briefly. Divide into two equal parts and flatten each into a round measuring about 7 inches in diameter by ½ inch thick.

5. With a knife dipped in flour, score each round into eight equal wedges. Brush with the egg wash and score decoratively with a fork, if desired.

6. Sprinkle with the cinnamon-and-sugar mixture and bake for 15 minutes or until golden brown. Let the two rounds cool slightly on a rack and cut into eight wedges each.

16 scones

TOPPING

Egg wash (2 large egg yolks mixed with 2 tablespoons heavy cream or milk)

1 cup granulated sugar mixed with 1 teaspoon ground cinnamon

Add chai-flavored scones to your next afternoon tea menu and watch your guests revel in this new taste sensation.

chai pie

The combination of classic chai spices and all-American apple pie makes this a stunning addition to the holiday dessert table. This version was created by personal chef Carolyn Manzi.

1½ cups apple cider

½ cup brewed black Nilgiri tea

3 tablespoons arrowroot powder

2 tablespoons freshly squeezed lemon juice

2 teaspoons pure vanilla extract

½ teaspoon ground cinnamon

½ teaspoon ground ginger

½ teaspoon ground cardamom

3 pounds apples, peeled, cored, and sliced

⅓ cup packed dark brown sugar

Prepared or freshly made double-crust 8-inch pie shell

1. Boil the cider and tea over high heat until reduced to ½ cup. Allow to cool.

2. Preheat the oven to 450°F.

3. Combine the cooled tea-and-cider mix with all the remaining ingredients except the apples, sugar, and piecrust in a large bowl and stir.

4. Put the sliced apples in a separate bowl and coat with the sugar; add more sugar if necessary to coat the apples thoroughly. Stir the sugar-and-apple mix into the liquid.

5. Pour into the prepared piecrust. Cover with the top crust. Cut slits into the pastry top with a sharp knife. Place the pie on a baking sheet and bake for 15 minutes.

6. Reduce the oven temperature to 350°F and continue to bake the pie until golden brown, about 45 minutes. Cool. Serve with a ginger sauce, chai *ros malai* (quick "Indian" cream; see page 117), or *paneer* (see page 116).

10 servings

a tea lover's tour of india

Peeta hai hamesha chai!
(I always drink chai!)
— Traditional Hindi Saying

everyone who travels to India returns home transformed, altered in some way by the experience. Each gift from this awesome country is different, but certainly tea will be among the many lingering memories, and masala chais head the list of teas savored.

The triumvirate of teas from India grow mainly in the regions known as Darjeeling, Nilgiri, and Assam, and all of these teas are from varietals of the plants *Camellia sinensis* or *Camellia sinensis* var. *assamica*. What makes teas from these three areas taste so similar yet so different? The answer is twofold: how they are grown and how they are processed.

Theoretically, any tea grown anywhere in the world could be processed green, oolong, or black. Even the young buds can be processed as white tea, or the leaves aged as pu-erhs. However, not all teas lend themselves to all three processes; processing, as well as desired flavor in the cup, depends on location, altitude, weather (particularly the type and amount of rainfall), and the agricultural work.

No matter how ideal the weather, how perfect the location, or how careful the tea bushes are maintained and plucked, it is critical that the processing method be a viable combination of art and science. The level of skill and attention of the workers, in conjunction with well-designed and -maintained machines, can bring out the absolute best flavors of the tea leaves, develop a beverage that is so-so, or worse, ruin the tea. The same attention is paramount with tea leaves that are hand-manipulated in the old-style method of careful heating in stone woks.

Nonetheless, for the passionate tea drinker, the choices are increasing at an amazing rate.

A Traveler's Tale

A Tea Lover Finds Her Ultimate Cup

Even though my husband, Krish, and I have been away from our native India for almost sixteen years, we have only been able to visit home a few times. One such visit was in August 1991, the only vacation time available from our work. In India, August is usually the tail end of the monsoon season, with strong storms, days of heavy mist and rain, and lush, dripping green foliage everywhere.

That August was rare and delightful: The monsoon had started to drift away in the early part of the month, so when we arrived on the 9th, we were met by clear days of bright, hot sun rising up over the Kònòchenjunga Mountains just 40 miles across the blue-green valley.

It was also a time of political trouble between the Nepali residents of Darjeeling and the Bengalis. The Nepalis were agitating for a state separate from Bengal, to be called "Gurkhaland." Although this has since become a reality, leading to greater prosperity and a stable economy in Darjeeling, during our visit the agitation forced my family and I to take a circuitous route to Darjeeling.

Normally we would have taken a small sedan taxi to Darjeeling up the moderately wide paved road that winds gradually through the forests to emerge into open expanses of spreading tea estates all around the road: gnarled, stunted bushes, some dating back 150 to 200 years, but shiny and green leaved due to frequent plucking and pruning. You could step out of the taxi, walk over to a bush, pinch the leaf, and inhale a delightfully spicy, pungent fragrance.

Because of threatened political demonstrations on the road that year, though, we took a Land Rover taxi from Siliguri, the rail head from Calcutta at the base of the hills, up the Pankhabari road, which is only

SARRA BARAILY was born and raised in Mussoorie, India. She lives in Michigan with her husband, Krishna, a violin teacher who plays in the Kalamazoo and Battle Creek symphony orchestras, and her daughter, Anjuli, now eighteen and a university freshman majoring in voice performance. Sarra works for Michigan State University in the College of Human Medicine.

slightly wider than a bike path. The narrow road soon steepened to almost a 45-degree angle, forcing our vehicle to the limit.

The Pankhabari road is overgrown with bamboo and pine, cryptomeria and wild orchid, a truly adventurous jungle of a route. Despite the steep climb, we were exhilarated by the sun, by the luscious green rice-field valley stretching away below us as we made our way up into the coolness of the Himalayas, and by the anticipation of coming home.

Halfway up the hill the road suddenly leveled out into a bountiful tea estate. We were so close to the tea bushes that we could have stuck our hands out the windows and plucked a few leaves. Getting thirsty and tired of riding in the bucking jeep, we casually asked our driver if he knew of any tea stall nearby. He nodded diffidently and a few minutes later braked with a rush beside an impossibly small wooden shed built over the *khud* (hillside) of shining green tea bushes stretching for what seemed to be miles.

A cheerful Nepali woman appeared at the window of the shed. When we asked if she had some hot tea, she smiled broadly, reached in front of her and opened the window further to display glass jars full of hard candy, biscuits, and tea. Behind her we could see a teakettle on a brazier, already beginning to steam.

The soft whistle of a steaming kettle of water is the most soothing, comforting sound in the world.

Lowering our heads to get through the small door opening, we made our way to the back of the shed, delicately held up by wooden stakes so as not to obstruct the growth of the tea bushes. We sat down on wooden stools and the tea lady brought in a tray of hot milk, grainy sugar, large chipped porcelain cups, and a teapot of the best Darjeeling tea I remember ever having: freshly picked large tea leaves that unfurled slowly in just-boiled water with a fragrance and taste that rivaled anything else in the world.

In this rare moment we were happy captives of tea's beauty and magic: the smiling face of the woman; the driver and my husband speaking softly in that lovely language of Nepali; Anjuli, our then eleven-year-old daughter, melting back into her childlike self, gazing around with wide, accepting eyes; and I watching and feeling it all, not able to say a word from the pleasure of realizing we were *home*.

The teapot drained, we continued on up the hill to the waiting arms of our family.

growing and processing techniques

The growing of teas depends upon altitude, climate, soil, and the attentive plucking of the leaves at just the right time of the year. Processing generates three basic categories of tea: *greens,* which are barely withered, and not oxidized or fired at all; *oolongs,* which are partially fired, retaining much moisture; and *black teas,* which are 100 percent fired. Greens taste grassy and fresh; oolongs are intensely and naturally perfumed and sweet; blacks are crisp and sharp and cleansing on the palate. To tea lovers these are but generalities because teas change from plucking to plucking, from season to season, and from area to area, making the lure of the leaf as intoxicating as the lure of the grape is to the wine connoisseur.

Other tea categories are *whites* and *yellows,* both made from the small, tender buds of high-quality tea plants; these have a delicate sweet taste and pale color in the cup. Whites and yellows are rare in India, and more common in China, although some white Assams have come to market and provide a remarkable cup. There is a sixth category of tea, an intentionally aged tea called *pu-erh,* made primarily in China. In India aged Darjeelings, called vintage teas, offer a unique and complex taste in the cup.

The process of drying leaves, molding them into myriad shapes — such as pellets, pearls, or smooth elegant leaves — then oxidizing them in special ovens is more art than craft, and perhaps the most fascinating attraction of tea besides its taste. Machinery does most of the work these days in India, but many estates still provide hand-processed teas in limited quantities.

darjeeling — the champagne of teas

One of the three primary tea-growing regions in India, Darjeeling is a beautiful area in northeastern India, south of Sikkim. Surrounded by the majestic snow-covered Kònòchenjunga Mountains in the foothills of the Himalayas, Darjeeling's the lucky recipient of heavy white clouds that continually mist the tea bushes.

To describe the flavor and style of Darjeeling teas without mentioning the phenomenon of location is impossible, because the soil, elevation (often as high as 6,500 feet), and weather (heavy rainfall and at least five hours of sun a day are necessary) count as much as the planting, plucking, and processing.

For many years I avoided Darjeelings, believing they were too astringent for my taste. Then a Darjeeling tea enthusiast suggested that I prepare this Indian nectar in the Chinese style, with hot water (190–200°F), steeping for 2 to 3 minutes only in a covered Chinese-style cup. Ah, now I understood the passion. Darjeeling is truly a flower in a cup, delicately perfumed, exquisite flavor notes, enormously satisfying.

As with any variety, Darjeelings vary from estate to estate and the choices are vast. (There are now eighty-six estates, producing about 11 million kilograms of tea annually.)

Most fine Darjeelings are sold by the season in the best grades and in whole leaves. A first flush is picked just after winter, usually from March through April, when the leaves are naturally spring-tender and lighter and greener in appearance. The second flush, perhaps the most sought after for its "muscatel" flavor, has a red-brown color with a slightly fruity taste. This is picked usually during May and June. The rain teas, picked generally from July through September, have an astringent yet bright taste. Autumnals are plucked in the fall, generally between October and November, and these teas are considerably more mellow in taste and character.

Two lesser known areas grow some commendable teas: the Dooars and Terai. Teas from the low-grown Dooars fall between the strength of an Assam and the delicacy of a Darjeeling. Teas from the plains of Terai offer a spicier bite than their Darjeeling relatives, and blend well with other teas. They take well to milk.

A Chinese covered cup, or guywan, is my favorite way to savor Darjeeling tea.

Teas like those in the Terai or Dooars may share some of the flavor characteristics of Darjeelings, but without the exceptional elevation and weather of the foothills of the Himalayas these teas never can duplicate the exquisite flavor, aroma, or even color of the finest Darjeelings.

Some tasters categorize Travancore tea with Darjeelings. This is actually a southern Indian tea that tastes more like a Ceylon, but some tea sellers classify it as a Darjeeling because of its similar astringency. It has a strong, full body that takes well to milk.

Whenever you can, try to purchase your Darjeelings from reputable tea shops that carry single-estate teas. Most commercial Darjeelings are blends (and many good ones at that), but to truly "taste Darjeeling" you must try single-estate teas. They are an investment in pure pleasure. For a complete list of the gardens of Darjeeling, see the list on pages 145–146.

A TRAVELER'S TALE

Sharing his impressions of Darjeeling is Mike Olsen, co-owner of Time for Tea, a tea salon in Philadelphia, Pennsylvania, which sells bulk teas from around the world, and in particular, fine Darjeelings.

A Tea Shop Owner Visits Darjeeling

How many ways are there to describe Darjeeling? Perhaps as many as there are languages in India. For me, my lasting impression is of standing on the foothills of the Himalayas watching the clouds pass below, feeling the magic that is Darjeeling.

The first thing you notice upon arrival at a tea estate is the aroma of the verdant tea bushes. Tea's musky, rich scent is noticeable whether it is pouring down rain or a perfectly clear day. You notice it most as you approach the fields. (At home, you can approximate the intoxicating atmosphere if you hold your nose right down into freshly brewed tea leaves.) The smell is one of so many things you take with you when you leave Darjeeling.

Without a doubt Darjeeling is one of the most beautiful places in the world. From the plains of the Dooars, to the steep slopes of the midranges, to the rolling hills at the higher altitudes, the land is an ocean of green. No wonder it's referred to in Indian folk tales as the land of thunderbolts or land of the dancing mists. The geography alone is worthy of legends.

Everything comes together in Darjeeling. The mountains are placed to funnel the proper air currents, which in turn bring the rain clouds at the right time of year. The sun fills the slopes with the proper amount of light each day. Clouds drift through, providing the humidity for the tea plants. Mother Nature prepared this land, yet when humans took an innocent bush and began to cultivate it, the combination became what perfection can be.

We are all beneficiaries of this serendipitous combination of Mother Nature's canvas and the tea planter's vision.

makaibari — the shining jewel

Within a land of superlatives is a small shining emerald with a name that means "place of corn," Makaibari Tea Estate. Arriving at this estate, near the town of Kurseong, was a relief after a week of the 117°F days in Delhi. The weather was perfect during this first week of June when it was only in the 70s and the threat of monsoons was weeks away.

Makaibari Tea Estate is truly a wonder. Heavily forested, it hosts the widest biodiversity of any tea plantation in the world with 2 acres of tropical forest per acre of tea and a staggering array of flora and fauna. On several occasions I was warned not to be eaten by tigers, and I suspect that my hosts were only half joking. Makaibari's owners have an extraordinary commitment to the land. As a result, they produce tea as pure as any you will taste, a golden jewel in a cup.

The Banerjee family, owners of Makaibari for several generations, provides jobs, schools, land to grow food, and a safe environment for the tea pickers and their families. Managers are not remote or standoffish; they and the pickers know one another and work together to create a tea that is truly special, the only organic, purely biodynamically grown tea in the world.

The majestic Darjeeling mountains appear to rise out of the mist.

making darjeeling tea

The amount of work that goes into making a pot of tea is mind-boggling. A general familiarity with tea production doesn't prepare you for what you see in person. After praying that the weather cooperates for the best possible growing conditions, tea producers begin the delicate art of processing.

On a very basic level, tea production involves the manipulation of water: first providing it, then taking it away at critical points. Water is needed to nourish the tea plant; later it is removed in the processing of the harvested leaves; then the tea must be protected from water during its transport and storage; finally, once it is delivered to the consumer, water is again added to bring the tea leaves back to "life."

Tea must be picked at the proper time. It will not wait for you. The tea is picked with care, primarily by women. It is generally held that women have a much better connection to the earth and work harder than men, but it also may be true that wages paid to women are sometimes lower than those paid to men. Some other jobs are considered more "important," and, thus, should be done by men.

The tea is transported to withering bins and spread 6 inches deep on screens before processing. Air is circulated, and the temperature is regulated depending on the humidity and how much moisture is to be removed from the tea. Then the tea is off to the rolling machines to undergo two separate rollings with a rest period between. After twenty minutes or so in drying machines, the tea is sent through a room of great shaking belts, screens, and chutes, which separate the leaves by size.

The tea harvested from each plot of land is processed separately, and tasted on a daily basis. It is a fascinating experience to taste the same tea several days in a row, to see how its character develops. Different leaves are blended to achieve maximum potential of the projected taste in the cup. Then the tea is again allowed to rest before it is shipped off to reveal itself to the consumer.

Any stage of the production can alter the flavor of the tea, and the utmost care must be taken. Tea is a forgiving plant . . . as long as you give it *constant* attention. A bad call at any stage will produce something unpalatable.

changes in flavor profiles

The flavor of Darjeeling has changed; today's Darjeeling is distinctively different than in years past. The axiom that a good Darjeeling tea is an astringent, intense brew is no longer valid. Teas that were produced from a hard wither for Russian palates in the 1970s and 1980s are now being made for a much more sensitive palate. Individual flavors are discernible, allowed to flourish. Each year brings more complex, fascinating teas.

The plant itself is changing, too, as a result of interplanting, clonals, and other techniques used to develop a better leaf on the bush for a better, more consistent taste in the cup. Tea cuttings were first brought to India from China by Robert Fortune and planted throughout Darjeeling. These smaller, tender Chinese plants were unable to fend off such foes such as red spider, green fly, and mold. Clonal varieties of the Assam plant, cultivated to be hardier, produce more, and have a shorter growing time, have been added to Darjeeling estates to make those teas healthier. As a result, the classic Darjeeling flavor has slowly changed.

Despite its fragility, the finer-leaf Chinese variety is still used to give Darjeeling its outstanding flavor, the bright, intense wash around the mouth. To make the tea bushes healthier (and more resistant to bugs), some estates plant with a higher ratio of Assam to Chinese plants. The two varieties of tea bushes grow together in the fields but are kept separate all the way through processing, to be blended to the taste of the tea maker. Darjeelings with the taste of Assam have the added benefits of a rich red tint and a fuller flavor in the final cup.

One exception to this trend is the Makaibari Tea Estate, which replants tea bushes in the traditional ratio and plants with seedlings and clonals only. This is quite time consuming and difficult, but worth the results in the cup. Makaibari also uses nothing unnatural on its biodynamically grown tea plants: no pesticides, no chemicals, nothing that is not natural.

The processing of tea into greens and oolongs in addition to the conventional blacks is a major shift among Darjeeling growers. Some estates are producing green and oolong varieties in skyrocketing amounts, with brilliant results — so much so that on several estates Chinese oolong makers are studying the production methods in Darjeeling. The oolongs are full of honey on the nose and in the cup. The greens are full of peach, apricot, and other fruit flavors. (A century ago producing greens was the typical processing method for Indian tea, but as demand for tea has grown, processing tea into blacks has become more common. Blacks last longer, travel better, and blend well with blacks from other countries.)

Tea plantations are some of the most beautiful areas in all of India.

Darjeeling is such a mystical land, it is no surprise that it produces such an outstanding tea. When we visit beautiful areas of the world, we can't help but leave something behind that will eventually draw us back. Those of us who've been to Darjeeling don't talk about someday, but about which day we will return to the people who live among the clouds.

cardamom tea

Cardamom is an essential spice in masala chai, but chai also tastes great when cardamom is its sole spice. Try this recipe with a delicately aromatic Darjeeling. I've added a touch of orange for fragrance, but you can omit it.

Boil the water with the orange peel and cardamom pods. Infuse for about 10 minutes. Add the tea, and infuse for 4 to 6 minutes more. Strain and serve with hot milk and sugar, as desired.

4 servings

6¾ cups water

1 3-inch strip fresh orange peel

12 crushed whole green cardamom pods

3 tablespoons black Darjeeling tea leaves

Loose-leaf teas, whether black or green, are the premier choices for the best-tasting chais.

debby lovell's chai meringues

3 large egg whites

1 cup sugar

½ teaspoon ground cardamom

¼ teaspoon ground cinnamon

¼ teaspoon ground cloves

Debby is a chai enthusiast who contributed this modified recipe to Gary and Jan Routh's chai Web page. They're light and dainty and contain zero fat. *Serve with your favorite Darjeeling. Adding a puree of fresh fruit on top is a delectable touch.*

1. Preheat the oven to 250°F.

2. Beat the egg whites with an electric mixer at low speed until foamy, then continue to beat at high speed until they form stiff peaks. You should be able to turn the bowl sideways without the egg whites moving.

3. Add the sugar to the egg whites a little at a time while continuing to beat at high speed. Turn off the mixer. Add the spices all at once and beat in gently by hand.

4. Drop the mixture into small mounds on baking sheets that have been covered with foil or parchment paper and bake for 90 minutes. Turn off the oven. Leave the meringues inside to sit overnight.

5. Remove from the pan gently and store in an airtight container.

3 dozen cookies

orange drops

Butter cookies, shortbread, and biscotti are excellent accompaniments to Indian tea, especially Darjeeling. Here is a favorite recipe of mine.

1. Preheat the oven to 350°F. Lightly grease two cookie sheets.
2. In a bowl cream together the butter, sugar, and orange zest until the mixture is fluffy. Add the orange juice concentrate and vanilla. Mix in the eggs, stirring until well blended.
3. In a separate bowl, sift together the flour, baking powder, and salt. Blend the dry ingredients into the moist ingredients.
4. Using a teaspoon, drop the dough onto the cookie sheets. Press an almond half into each cookie. Bake for 12 to 15 minutes, until golden brown.

3 dozen cookies

The pungent flavor of chai makes an excellent companion to these orange-and-almond cookies.

½ cup (1 stick) unsalted butter, at room temperature

½ cup sugar

Zest from 2 oranges (about 2 tablespoons)

2 tablespoons orange juice concentrate, at room temperature

1 teaspoon pure vanilla extract

2 large eggs, lightly beaten

2 cups all-purpose flour

2½ teaspoons baking powder

¼ teaspoon salt

1 cup almond halves

assam — the hearty one

It is quite probable that you have already had an Assam tea, or a blend with "the hearty one" in it. More tea is produced in the Indian state of Assam than in most tea-growing countries of the world. The tea plants are also different from Chinese varieties or those grown elsewhere in India. They are *Camellia sinensis* var. *assamica,* a broad-leaf, hardy evergreen species that has become the most reliable tea bush in the world, capable of withstanding infestations of bugs better than other tea varietals, and able to endure the rains so common to this area.

But how it grows is not nearly as important as how it cups, and Assam tastes terrific. It's rich and full of heavy body, some fragrance, and a bite that can stand up to milk and flavorings yet does not have the astringency so common in Darjeeling or even Ceylon teas.

Assam is excellent for blending because it adds body to those teas with thinner tastes but great fragrance, and offers other flavor notes to give any blend a more balanced, more interesting flavor profile. This is not to say that Assam is not a stand-alone tea, for it is indeed. For many people Assam *is* tea, and it is black tea. All these qualities also make Assam the number one choice for masala chai lovers, who realize that the richness of this tea makes it ideal to blend with strong spices.

Smooth, hearty black Assam teas offer strong tea flavor that stands up well to the most exotic spices and creamiest milks.

In the early history of tea in India, all tea was processed as green tea. Soon, however, merchants as well as tea growers realized that green tea, no matter how well it is processed, has a very short life span. If a vendor has more tea than customers, there go the profits. So, like the Chinese, Indian tea processors began processing their tea into blacks to achieve longer transportation schedules and longer shelf life. This has now become the predominant category of Indian tea.

Ironically, as more and more connoisseurs have made their presence known in today's market, more manufacturers have become willing to take the risk of making green, and even white teas from Assams. These greens and whites are not nearly as elegant as their Chinese relatives but do offer the palate a remarkable sensation — a multilayered taste profile that should be experienced.

For the finest black Assams, look for golden "tips": points at the ends of the leaves that are golden, indicating fine processing. For greens and whites, look for even coloring and finely shaped leaves. For the heartiest flavors and the purest tastes, full or partially broken leaves are the best. Good Assams are available in all grades, but as always, the final arbiter is not the look of the leaf or its fragrance, but its taste in the cup.

india's spice treasures

Fifteenth-century explorer Vasco da Gama reportedly requested a cutting of a pepper stalk from the potentate of Calicut (Kerala) to take back to Spain. Allegedly, the calm reply was, "Certainly, take our pepper. Alas, you can not take our rains." This was a sly reference to the importance of the region's twin monsoons, which are essential to the prized pepper plant's survival.

A Traveler's Tale

A Tea Blender Visits Assam

This tale was shared by Michael Harney of Harney & Sons Teas. Michael is a graduate of the Cornell University School of Hotel and Restaurant Administration, and is the Harney company's primary buyer of tea. His father, John Harney, founded the firm.

Driving by car down the whole of Assam is amazing. Assam is not a tourist place; it's hotter and sunnier, with spots that are the wettest on earth from the relentless rains. It's not unusual to see tea plantations covered with 3 feet of water from the heavy pourings of the season.

From the Dibrugarh Airport, we started our trek to Gauhati in southwestern Assam, where I had come to buy teas. The roads were rough, the travel not easy, dodging cows, dogs, and people along the way, but what a sight the tea fields were at the end of the journey: lush, lush green, the visible result of all that rain, with eucalyptus shade trees popping up here and there among the thousands of tea bushes.

The huge, wide, slow-moving water of the famous Brahmaputra River does not abut the tea farms (it flows a few miles away), but it's quite a sight to see how the river changes from its flat beginning in the north of India to its mountainous swing up to China and Tibet. I remember looking at it from the airplane and thinking it was like a magnificent silver ribbon cutting through this emerald green region called Assam.

We arrived at the first tea farm about closing time, when the women tea pluckers were walking away from their task of picking the very large Assam leaves. They wore the most beautiful saris, gorgeous silks of vibrant colors accented with yellows to catch the sun. They moved as gracefully as trained dancers despite the precarious balancing requirements of a tower of items on their heads: wide-brimmed hats, heavy baskets full of tea leaves, and on top of that umbrellas for the constant rains. It was a breathtaking introduction to Assam.

The tea pluckers there have a very complex job, enduring the volleying sun and rain almost daily and certainly through much of each day they work. However, because the leaves of the Assam plants are so big, these women can pluck them more easily than the smaller Chinese varieties in Darjeeling — they can fill up their baskets quicker and fill more baskets per day. Still, it's such hard work that we could not help but admire such tenacity and diligence.

processing assam tea

The long, flat fields of the Assam farms we visited were fragrant with the sweet malty smell of fresh tea leaves. The heat and dampness of the fields provided a surprisingly sensual experience; the fragrance was intoxicating in the gardens, and in the facility where the withering (drying) and processing are performed. It was tea heaven.

It was quite fascinating to watch the crush, tear, curl (CTC) pellet machine where the bright green fresh leaves traveled the long, long conveyer in its slow travel for at least an hour. Oxidizing along the way, the green leaves turned brown naturally along this 100-foot path, as a cut apple would when exposed to the air. Then the lightly withered leaves were placed into a special oven to oxidize a full 100 percent. (Green tea is not oxidized at all, and oolongs are oxidized 2 to 80 percent, depending on their various styles; all blacks are oxidized 100 percent.)

In the processing of Assam tea, leaves are often intentionally cut up because they are so large. They sometimes require the additional step of filtering with a cylinder sieve. If the leaves are not small

The tea pluckers balance large baskets on their heads. Throughout the day, they will collect several baskets full of leaves.

enough to sift through, they are run through a machine again to break them into smaller pieces.

Unlike Darjeeling tea leaves, Assams are generally processed by the CTC method to accommodate the enormous demand from India itself. India's taste is for CTC tea, which is cheaper, is plentiful, and lasts longer.

The market for loose, full-leaf teas is always risky. These teas have a shorter life span and so must be sold more quickly and drunk sooner than the long-lived CTC tea. And as in any agricultural business, the need for freshness makes all produce vulnerable, even a dried leaf like tea. Still, you can pay almost as much for a high-quality, uncut, loose-leaf Assam as the finest Darjeeling. The quality, I am happy to report, is improving continually, and the potential for even better teas in the future is enormous. So the inspiration to create fine Assams remains.

Tea leaf plucking is a complex job requiring concentration, stamina, and skilled hands.

the pleasures of assam

Assam is well known as a good blender that offers lots of body. Its fragrance is less intense than other Indian teas, particularly Darjeeling, but the honey flavor in the best Assams more than compensates for the lack of aroma. The familiar maltiness in the medium grades is satisfying and continues to be very popular.

Exceptionally fine cloning has created intensely rich Assams with beautiful gold tips, especially on the Jay Shree Gardens (Meleng,

Towkok, and Nahorhabi). These pretty gold-and-black teas offer a taste that is not too astringent with good body, some of the best Assam has to offer. Assam is my tea of choice for the morning; I especially like the Nahorhabi, and I drink it plain. These teas are perfection the way they are, so why mess with perfection?

Assam is very approachable, the black tea most people know best, and certainly one of the best-selling loose teas our company markets and the most popular Indian tea sold anywhere. We use a blend of Assam teas of both CTC and full-leaf manufacture to give our chai a heartier taste. Called Indian Spice Tea, it has a clear, clean note from cardamom and cardamom oil, and a spicy backdrop from cinnamon.

We've discovered that there is a big, enthusiastic market of people who like to add their own touch when making chai at home; this dried mixture is the perfect recipe for them. Consumers can make it as milky, as sweet, and as fresh as they desire, and if they like other spices, they can add whatever suits their mood.

4 cups water

1 cinnamon stick

1 1-inch piece ginger,
   peeled and cut into
   4 slices

12 green cardamom pods

4 teaspoons black
   Assam tea leaves

1 cup milk

assam
spice chai

1. Combine the water and spices in a saucepan over medium heat and bring to a boil.

2. Reduce the heat to low, cover, and simmer for 20 minutes.

3. Add the tea and milk and simmer over low heat for 3 more minutes.

4. Strain through a fine sieve and pour into prewarmed cups (see page 7) immediately. Add sugar to taste.

4 cups

cardamom cookies

These delicately scented cookies are an unusual and addictive twist on the traditional sugar cookies. Buy only the best green cardamom pods and grind them yourself for the best results. White cardamom makes the dough whiter but the whitener comes from bleaching. I think the light flavor of cardamom fills up all the senses, making these the perfect accent to the rich, satisfying cup of any Assam.

1. Preheat the oven to 400°F.

2. Sift the flour, sugar, and cardamom into a bowl. Add the butter and work it into the dry ingredients with a pastry blender. Blend in the egg, vanilla, and milk and stir until a dough is formed.

3. Shape the dough into ½-inch balls and place them on an ungreased cookie sheet. Flatten each ball with the bottom of a glass, covered with a damp cloth. Sprinkle the cookies with additional granulated sugar and bake for 6 to 8 minutes.

6 dozen cookies

2 cups sifted all-purpose flour

1 cup sugar

2 tablespoons ground cardamom seeds

¾ cup (1½ sticks) unsalted butter

1 large egg, slightly beaten

1 teaspoon vanilla extract

1 tablespoon whole or 2% milk

nilgiri — the fragrant one

In the south of India stand the fragrant Blue Mountains, or Nilgiris, redolent with the scent of tea bushes, thousands of blue gum cypresses, and even more eucalyptus trees. The latter are so popular that eucalyptus oil, used for many medical applications, is known as Nilgiri oil.

Nilgiri teas have established themselves as a third choice in the triumvirate of Indian teas, but they have not received the prestige of Darjeeling nor reached the huge production of Assam teas, although that gap is closing. Of the three tea-producing regions Nilgiri has the highest production per capita, because more of its land mass is devoted to tea farms than is Assam's. The potential to outstrip Assam in overall production certainly exists.

The natural lovely fragrance of Nilgiri teas has always been considered important in blends. It was not until the late twentieth century, however, that Nilgiri teas developed the significance they now have as stand-alone teas (like Darjeelings).

Nilgiris are like good everyday table wines: reliable, with good color and a heavy nose. They fall between the two extremes of Indian tea, the hearty Assams and the delicate Darjeelings.

For decades much of the production from the Nilgiri region was sold to locals, to the Russians, and to Iran and Iraq, Saudi Arabia, and Egypt, all of whom favor the rich, dark CTC (crush, tear, curl) teas. Nilgiri tea appeals to these cultures because of its strong taste, dark color, increased caffeine, and ability to stand up to milk.

Russia's economy is so fragile that its people can no longer afford the orthodox Nilgiris that used to make up 50 percent of their purchases; indeed, they barely can afford the lower-priced CTC. Russia's loss is now America's gain. The versatility of Nilgiri tea means that tea lovers can choose between delicate orthodox teas from high-end estates and stronger CTC teas from the small farms throughout the region.

Nilgiris are ideal for experimentation, creating popular oolong and green varieties that never spoil in the cup from oversteeping. Nilgiri's innate ability not to cloud, to always proffer a clear and vivid color, makes it the perfect choice for what makes up 85 percent of the U.S. tea market: iced tea.

Nilgiri teas have another attribute: Their soft flavor makes them wonderful foils for flavorings, scents, and fruits. Such teas easily constitute 35 percent of the hot-tea market in the United States.

Assam teas are great in tea bags or for making fresh chai at home, but Assam does not fare as well in liquid concentrates, which

All good chais start with a brew of hot, strong, and fragrant tea.

sometimes become bitter upon reheating. Fortunately for manufacturers and the increasing numbers of consumers who want easy liquid concentrates, Nilgiri tea is being used more and more for its goof-proof preparation. Reheating is no problem — the flavor of the spices is kept intact and the tea taste remains authentic because Nilgiri teas are hard to overbrew. What could be better than a tea that's mellow in the cup whether used in single-estate form, in a blend, or as a tea in a masala chai?

Years of planting with clonals of Darjeeling bushes and the area's naturally good soil quality have provided today's Nilgiris with vibrant color, a satisfying taste in the cup, and a signature heavy yet exquisite fragrance.

A low-elevation tea like a Nilgiri can never have the delicacy of Darjeelings, which are grown at very high altitudes. Instead, the

In the sky there sounds
the comely drums of the
  gods,
and there blew a pleasant
  wind
bearing a heavenly
  fragrance.

— VALMIKI, FROM
  "RAMAYANA"

lower altitude and the lack of weather extremes found in Assam and Darjeeling provide a more consistent and richer tea in Nilgiri. Another plus is that the Nilgiri area receives light rainfall compared to the extreme monsoons of the north, which provides more pluckings per year.

Unlike the gigantic estates found in Assam and Darjeeling, most Nilgiri plantings are found on small farms of between 5 and 50 hectares. The farmers do not process the tea themselves; instead, tea manufacturers have built factories nearby, to process the leaves by the CTC method. Each factory processes the leaves of from ten to thirty farmers, and handles the sales.

Nilgiri teas are grown primarily in the Annamalais, the High Ranges, the Peerumedu-Vandiperiyar belt, Karnataka, and Wynaad in Keral. The Nilgiri region's many high-end estates include Tiger Hill, Craigmore, and Burnside; these process right on the estate, resulting in fine full-leaf teas prepared in the orthodox manner. Such orthodox Nilgiri teas command higher prices each year. Their reputations for a more delicate taste and lighter color in the cup — ironically similar to the high-grown Darjeelings — are also growing.

Today more than ever Nilgiris are shedding their underdog status as more and more tea blenders and manufacturers recognize their good value and ability to blend with popular fruit scents and flavors. They also brew easily and with great flavor, either hot or iced, and you can choose between a dark rich cup from CTC processing and a delicate taste from orthodox manufacture of the fragrant one, Nilgiri tea. In 1998 the first organic Nilgiris were exported to the United States, another signal that these teas are rising in quality and value. See page 146 for a list of top Nilgiri gardens.

iced nilgiri chai

1. In a medium saucepan, boil the water and pour it over the tea. Return the mixture to the saucepan, add the spices, and simmer for about 10 minutes. Strain and cool.

2. Mix with milk and sugar to taste and pour over ice, preferably cubes made out of tea to prevent dilution. Ice cubes made of lemonade or any favorite juice are also great with iced teas.

4 servings

4 cups water

4 heaping teaspoons black Nilgiri tea

½ teaspoon ground cardamom

½ teaspoon ground cinnamon

¼ teaspoon freshly grated ginger

A clear, vibrant, beautiful beverage is the reliable result of iced teas brewed with Nilgiri leaves.

¾ cup chopped blanched unsalted almonds

1 quart whole milk

1 quart brewed chai

⅓ cup basmati rice, washed

¾ cup sugar (adjust downward if your brewed chai is sweetened)

1 teaspoon rose water

¼ teaspoon cardamom seeds (from whole cardamom pods), crushed

chai khir
chai rice pudding

This spin on rice pudding has as many variations as there are cuisines in India, but the trick to the authenticity is using basmati rice. It's a tad more expensive, but worth it. The lovely fragrance of a pudding made with basmati is an exquisite complement to the lingering fragrance of a fine Nilgiri. A "scent-sational" way to have dessert and tea.

1. Toast the almonds in the oven by spreading them on a baking sheet and toasting under the broiler for about 2 minutes. Set aside.

2. Bring the milk to a boil over high heat, stirring to prevent a skin from forming on the surface. Reduce the heat to moderate and stir occasionally for about 30 minutes. Add the brewed chai.

3. Add the rice and continue cooking, stirring frequently, for about 30 minutes more or until the grains of rice are softened.

4. Add the sugar and ½ cup of the chopped almonds and stir over low heat until pudding is thick enough to coat a wooden spoon thickly (about 15 minutes). Reserve the remaining almonds.

5. Take the pan off the heat and stir in the rose water and cardamom seeds. Pour the pudding into a shallow 7 by 12-inch baking dish, spreading smoothly and evenly.

6. Refrigerate for at least 4 hours or until the pudding is firm to the touch and thoroughly chilled. Sprinkle the remaining toasted almonds on top.

6 servings

side trip —the magnificent taj mahal

The lovely scents of fresh flowers are everywhere inside the Taj Mahal, offerings from natives and tourists who make the pilgrimage to see this monument to enduring love of the Mogul Emperor Shah Jahan for his wife, born Arjumand Banu Behum yet known to all as Mumtaz Mahal, Ornament of the Palace.

The acoustics inside are incredible. A false dome that rests in the secondary structure gives delicate reverberations whenever visiting Muslims recite the thirty-sixth chapter of the Quran, which is beautifully carved on the four main doorways of the structure in a permanent display of this traditional deathbed prayer.

Although the shah employed designers and architects, his own imprint is on the building that now rises along the banks of the river Yamuna. The grieving shah designed an identical building in black marble for himself to be placed on the opposite side of the river, but his son did not honor that wish; instead, he placed a modest gravestone for his father near the tomb of his mother, who died in 1631 giving birth to her fourteenth child. (She and the shah are actually buried in a crypt below her magnificent tomb.)

Shah Jahan had a romantic soul and genuine love for his wife, and the Taj Mahal is an eternal edifice to her memory. Still, his devotion to its construction, which he supervised from 1631 to 1654, verged on obsession.

For the twenty thousand craftsmen from central Asia and India who worked on this monument to love over twenty-two years, praise and money could not possibly have been enough payment. All met with a harsh fate: The shah had their fingers severed so that nothing like the Taj Mahal could ever be built again.

If there is one place on the face of the earth where all the dreams of living men have found a home from the earliest day when man began the dream of existence, it is India.

— ROMAIN ROLLAND

the
taj mahal

You allowed your kingly power to vanish, Shajahan,
but your wish was to make imperishable a teardrop of love.

Time has no pity for the human heart,
he laughs at its sad struggle to remember.

You allured him with beauty, made him captive,
and crowned the formless death with fadeless form.

The secret whispered in the hush of night to the ear
of your love is wrought in the perpetual silence of stone.

Though empires crumble to dust, and centuries are lost in shadows,
the marble still sighs to the stars, "I remember."

"I remember." — But life forgets, for she has her call to the Endless:
and she goes on her voyage unburdened,
leaving her memories to the forlorn forms of beauty.

— RABINDRANATH TAGORE

A Traveler's Tale

A Tourist Visits the Taj Mahal

Who could travel to India and not view that magnificent monument to love, the Taj Mahal?

My friend and I had seen so many exotic sights on our travels through India, many of them recommended by friends with enormous (and justified) enthusiasm. Their voices would change to a quiet, almost reverential tone when recalling the man-made treasure in the city of Agra. Some extolled the romantic virtues of the Taj Mahal under the moonlight, others were mesmerized by its blaze of color at sunset, still others thought the magnificent tomb was more exciting at sunrise. My friend and I opted for the latter and set our alarm for 3:30 A.M. before we went to bed at our modest hotel, yet we barely slept a wink thinking of our impending adventure.

We left the room at 4 A.M., and quickly realized that getting out of the hotel was our first challenge. It was locked tight, with no one on duty to unlock the gates. Locking the hotel gave both guests and staff a feeling of security during the night, but no one realized how difficult it would be to leave.

Determined, we climbed the nearly 8-foot-high fence, and climbed down again when on the other side. We felt like burglars, although real ones usually break *into* a hotel, not out.

Indian cities are rarely quiet. Every street in every city seems to be constantly teeming with people, slow-moving cows, lumbering trucks, taxis, and tricycle-style rickshaws kicking up dust with every move. This moment before dawn brought a remarkable stillness . . . and no rickshaws. Determined to see the man-made marvel, we decided to hit the dust and walk the 5-mile route to the Taj Mahal.

Terre Pasero, who lives in California, is an educator and seminar leader who teaches the skills needed to embrace diversity in the workplace. She has lived in Japan and Spain, and has traveled to many places throughout the world.

Like a vision in the distance ahead of us came the curled body of an older Indian man, hunched over the handlebars of his pedicab in a gesture that warded off the freezing early-morning chill and gave him the appearance of a determined bicycle racer whose every breath sent steam into the air in front of him. He knew no English, but understood the words "Taj Mahal," so we boarded his "rickety-shaw" and set off.

We arrived just in time for the sun to rise, yet nothing prepared us for the first glimpse of this magnificent mausoleum. Patterns of semiprecious gemstones, hand-set into the marble in specific patterns, caused the pristine white exterior to shimmer in the morning light. It was magic. Its overwhelming perfection hyp-notized us, commanded us to be still as we sat before it for a long time, admiring the

The magical combination of tea and India has inspired writers from around the world.

reflecting pools, catching our breath at the shapes of the tomb, reminiscent of its Damascene origins, and thinking about how it came to be built by a man besotted with grief and love for his queen.

After our trip to amazement, my friend and I walked to a little café nearby, drank some warming chai, and basked in a sweet silence, allowing the exquisite beauty of viewing the Taj Mahal at sunrise to envelop us just a little longer until the hustle-bustle of another day in India began.

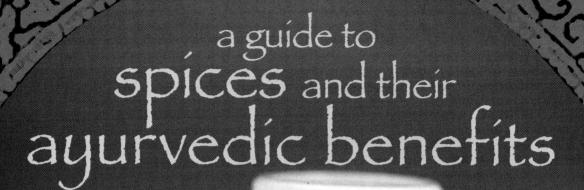

a guide to
spices and their
ayurvedic benefits

**He preferred to know the power of herbs
and their nature for curing purposes, and, heedless
of glory, to excercise that quiet art.**

— VIRGIL, *AENEID*

Chai is a wonderfully palate-pleasing drink that is also good for you. Most people know that the base of this drink, tea, is healthful, but few know that spices, too, have beneficial properties. Ayurveda, the ancient Indian system of holistic health care, suggests that a balance of spices and nutritious food can do much to improve overall health.

what is ayurveda?

In Sanskrit, *ayur* means "life" and *veda* means "knowledge," so Ayurveda is the "knowledge of how to live." The Ayurvedic system includes balance among the three *doshas* — the "humors" or waste products of digestion. These three humors are *kapha* (water or phlegm and earth), which controls body stability, lubrication, and potential energy; *pitta* (fire or bile and water), which controls the body's balance of kinetic and potential energies and involves digestion of food or "thoughts"; and *vata* (air or wind), which is the principle of kinetic energy in the body and controls the nervous system and body movement.

The *doshas* bind the elements of earth, air, fire, water, and wind. All are believed to help the normal growth of children and easy aging of adults. To be in complete balance with all three *doshas* is to be *tridoshic*.

The Ayurvedic suggestions for a good diet also incorporate ways to balance the basic six tastes: sweet or *madhura;* sour or *amla;* salty or *lavana;* astringent or *kasaya;* bitter or *tikta;* and pungent or *katur.*

Of course this brief description cannot do justice to the rich and ancient art of Ayurveda. If you'd like to learn more, take a look at the books listed in Recommended Reading on pages 121–122.

how to use the spice guide

All the following spice names are given in English, then Latin, unless otherwise noted. Common Indian names are also included in the text where applicable.

Unless otherwise noted, all of these spices should be purchased whole. Keep them in tightly sealed jars in a cool dark place. (Next to the stove is handy, but the warmth depletes the spices of their flavors.) Grate or crush them as needed. If whole spices are not available, purchase ground ones, but in very small quantities, and preferably from bulk containers rather than commercially packaged jars. Bulk spice grocers, especially Indian specialty markets, tend to turn over their inventory much quicker, providing you with a choice of fresher spices.

Generally, the spices used in masala chais are healthful for everyone. A pregnant or lactating woman, however, should seek counsel before making any herbal infusion or using an excess of any spice that could overstimulate to her system.

The Ayurvedic benefits listed below are not to be considered absolutes in the treatment of any illness. Should you have concerns about any symptoms, please see your medical practitioner; do not attempt to treat yourself with any herbs or spices without professional supervision.

For best results in creating or cooking with chais, always buy whole spices in small quantities, and store in a cool, dark cupboard.

spices and world trade

The exotic spices of India have played a vibrant role in the development of the Western world. They were one of the central reasons why Christopher Columbus set out from Spain to find India. He obviously, and ironically, never reached India but "discovered" the Americas instead, giving our native peoples the lasting misnomer "Indians." Columbus did bring back spices from the Caribbean and other stops along his misguided way, so Queen Isabella got some of her money's worth for the long voyage.

In the fifteenth and sixteenth centuries spices were the most sought-after items in the world, with the Dutch, Chinese, British, and, much later, Americans participating in this search for condiments. Perhaps the most important reason why Europeans coveted reliable sources for spices was that the refrigeration and freezing equipment so common today, as well as our sophisticated preservation methods, were not available. So it's easy to understand how attractive spices were to both professional and amateur chefs. The bite of coriander or cloves, the vibrance of pepper, the fragrance of cinnamon and other such spices were not only desirable but in fact essential in keeping foods palatable longer. Today spices are used less to preserve foods than to enhance them, to add a piquance that excites the palate or aids the digestion.

ajwain (omum)

(Carum copticuma)

A relative of caraway, it offers pungent and bitter seeds that can satisfy both *vata* and *kapha*.

How to Use. Crush the seeds and sprinkle them on top of your favorite milky chai recipe.

Ayurvedic Benefits. Ajwain is used primarily as a digestive or as a carminative and antiseptic. Seeds can be chewed and are excellent after dinner to alleviate indigestion, colic, or intestinal gas.

allspice
(Pimenta dioica)

allspice

A native of the Americas, allspice is aptly named, because it tastes like a combination of pepper, cinnamon, nutmeg, and cloves, yet has its own distinct flavor. The island of Jamaica still produces the bulk of these berries, which grow to the size of a pea on a large myrtle tree. The tree's small white flowers have a delicate aroma that infuses the bark, leaves, and berries themselves. The berries are harvested while green and then sun-dried to a brown color.

Prominent in Caribbean cuisine, allspice has been used by the Aztecs and Mayans. Allspice is also known as Jamaica pepper or myrtle pepper, and as *Pimenta dioica* or *Eugenia pimenta,* or the pimento tree. Other aromatic shrubs native to the West Indies bear similar names: Carolina allspice *(Calycanthus floridus);* wild allspice *(Lindera benzoin),* also known as spicebush or spice wood, fever bush, and allspice tree.

How to Use. Like most spices, allspice berries can be ground to a powder, but when used in chais allspice should always be freshly ground with a mortar and pestle or a pepper mill, to maintain its sharp taste and aroma.

Ayurvedic Benefits. Allspice is warming and therefore beneficial for blood circulation. It also aids digestion.

cardamom

cardamom

(Elettaria cardamomum)

This wonderfully fragrant spice comes in two varieties, green and black, but the shades of green range from white to very dark. Generally, the mellower black cardamom is added to savories, and the green to sweets. Because they are more pungent, green cardamom seeds work for all dishes.

Dark green indicates heavily dried pods, usually dried in an oven; light green pods are usually air-dried outside, and white is not at all a natural hue, but a result of bleaching with hydrogen peroxide. Ironically, white is the most expensive, and used by many bakers who like the fact that the whiteness blends in with flours to make a pretty dough that nonetheless takes on the exquisite scent of this spice. Avoid the powders or seeds for your chai drinks; instead, opt for lush green pods, which add the truest flavor without overwhelming the tea.

Black cardamom seeds, which are nearly 1 inch long (green seeds are about ¼ inch), are a botanical cousin but not truly cardamom. They are grown in Africa and dried in a style that lends them a smoky taste, often referred to by connoisseurs as a peppery taste. It is this black cardamom that is common to food in Pakistan and northern India, particularly Indian garam masala (a warm blend of spices; see page 115).

Although related to cardamom and with a similar aroma, the Melegueta pepper's tiny grains have a hot peppery taste. This spice is sometimes referred to as grains of Paradise and tastes great in Indian cuisine; it would overwhelm most chai mixes, though.

Hand harvesting helps make cardamom the third most expensive spice in the world (after saffron and vanilla). A member of the ginger family, it grows on a shrub usually 8 to 15 feet high, with long pointed leaves and short flowering stems.

Cardamom is grown primarily in Africa, yet the Malabar Coast of India is actually the world's largest producer. It also grows in Sri Lanka and recently has been cultivated in Mexico and throughout Central America. Guatemala, known for some of the finest cardamom in the world, has the Middle East as its biggest market, where the custom is to add cardamom to the acidic, thick Arab-style coffee that is so beloved.

Cardamom comes in pods, decorticated (whole seeds), or ground into a powder. Seeds and ground cardamom are considerably less expensive than the whole pods, which can cost upward of $70 per pound. Grinding pods and seeds lowers the price and also lowers the quality because the enemies of spices — air, humidity, heat — have a chance to rear their ugly heads. Starting from the whole pod guarantees a fresher, purer flavor and, ironically, may prove less expensive because there is less waste. Despite its high price, cardamom does offer a great deal of value, because a little goes a long way. Cardamom pods have a long shelf life when properly stored in tightly covered glass jars and placed in a cool, dry spot. Even a masala chai fiend can buy enough cardamom pods to last a year for under $10.

How to Use. Cardamom must be roasted to bring out its full flavor. To roast cardamom, remove the papery pods and then remove the seeds, which are brown-black and somewhat sticky. Heat a skillet (dry) and add the seeds, stirring them constantly with a wooden paddle until roasted, releasing their fragrance.

Ayurvedic Benefits. Cardamom has many digestive properties and acts as a breath freshener when chewed. It is frequently added to mulled wines and punches for an extra feeling of warmth. It has many benefits: It acts as a diuretic, an antigas or antinausea aid, an expectorant, and even, some say, an aphrodisiac. When added to chai, cardamom helps inhibits the mucus-forming properties of milk.

cinnamon

cinnamon

(Cinnamomum zeylanicum)

Native to Sri Lanka, cinnamon actually comes in two varieties: Sri Lankan or Ceylon cinnamon *(C. zeylanicum),* which grows from a small laurel evergreen tree, and cassia *(C. cassia,* known in Hindi as *dalchini).* Cinnamon was prominently mentioned in both Sanskrit manuscripts and the Bible; during the era of the great explorers in the fifteenth and sixteenth centuries, it became the most sought-after spice in the world.

Cinnamon comes from the tree's bark, which is pungent and sweet, yet very hot. The outer bark is peeled away from the branch and the inner bark is rolled up into a quill (or quillings) about 1 inch in diameter; this is the familiar rolled cinnamon stick. Cinnamon is available to use as sticks and as pieces of the bark itself. The twigs, pungent and sweet, are not as hot as the bark.

Most of the cinnamon available in the United States is the lower-priced cassia, which originated in Burma and is now cultivated extensively in southern China and Indonesia. Its quills are larger and coarser than cinnamon quills, and much less expensive than true cinnamon. However, cassia has less of the pungency and fire of Sri Lankan cinnamon.

How to Use. If you are using sticks, crush them prior to putting them into tea; ground cinnamon can be brewed with the tea itself but will not give as strong a flavor.

Ayurvedic Benefits. Cinnamon, which can lower blood sugar, may be useful for diabetics; it is also good for chills, the common cold, arthritis, and rheumatism. As an infusion, it is excellent for menstrual cramps and as a general bone tonic because of its warming properties.

cloves

(Syzygium aromaticum)

cloves

These natives of the Spice Islands (Moluccas) in Southeast Asia look like rusty nails in their dried, unopened flower-bud state. Now grown in Indonesia, Madagascar, Tanzania, Sri Lanka, Grenada, and Malaysia, they are pungent, warm, and strong yet slightly bitter. They're known in Hindi as *laung* or as *clavus* (which means "nail").

How to Use. Cooking tempers cloves' bitterness. Only one or two cloves are necessary to infuse a large pot of chai. Simply drop them in whole.

Ayurvedic Benefits. This pungent or *katu* spice increases *vata* and *pitta* and reduces *kapha*. It's excellent for chills, lethargy, or depression and for those who are overweight. It is a mild, warming digestive and used to treat neuromuscular degenerative disorders. Use sparingly.

coriander

(Coriandrum sativum)

coriander

A member of the carrot family, this herb (called *dhania* in Hindi) has pungent aromatic leaves, which are called Chinese parsley or cilantro, and is used extensively in the cuisines of China and Mexico. To flavor Indian chais use only coriander seeds, not the leaves. An ancient herb (mentioned in the Bible and even found in the tombs of the Egyptian pharaohs), coriander is very popular in northern Europe and in India's famous curries. Indian coriander seeds are very pungent yet sweet, not unlike the sweet/tart taste of a citrus peel.

How to Use. Coriander seeds taste best freshly roasted and ground.

Ayurvedic Benefits. A digestive, this herb has been noted to have cardiovascular benefits.

experimenting with spices

Cardamom, which comes in a pod that covers the seed, can actually be used whole for an incredibly delicate yet intoxicatingly perfumed tea. Try it in your finest Darjeeling. Cinnamon most often comes in powder form and adds fire to chai, but if you just want a hint of this spice serve the chai with the cinnamon stick on the side. The stick is stirred in the tea just a few times and produces a mild fiery taste. Fresh ginger is infinitely more pungent than powdered or crystallized ginger, and adds "wow" to your chai. Simply cut off one or two slices from a ginger root and pop it into the tea and spice mixture. Remove the ginger slices with a slotted spoon prior to serving.

fennel

(Foeniculum vulgare; F. officinale)

fennel

Candy-coated fennel seeds are a colorful digestive and breath freshener served after meals in Indian restaurants and private homes. Dried fennel seeds add a lively touch to chai recipes, particularly herbal ones. However, fennel chais do not have the exceptional warmth and fire that cinnamon or cloves contribute to the brew. The ancient Greeks thought that fennel would help reduce weight and referred to it as *marathron,* a verb meaning "to grow thin." It's known in Hindi as *saunf*.

How to Use. Crush fennel seeds or use them whole; add them to your chais at the last minute to get the most of the flavor.

Ayurvedic Benefits. Pungent and sweet, fennel helps the circulation, is an anti-inflammatory, and, especially for pregnant women, acts as a uterine stimulant. It also promotes milk flow in lactating women, which helps colicky babies.

ginger
(Zingiber officinale)

ginger

Known as green or root ginger (*adrak* in Hindi), this knobby root is a rhizome cultivated in Asia for more than three thousand years. Its clean, spicy flavor has been used for centuries in cooking throughout Asia. As early as the second century the Phoenicians recognized its medical properties and used ginger to calm stomach ills. Ginger was a popular commodity in ancient times, when the Chinese traded this root spice (and their prized silks) to the Romans.

Today ginger is grown throughout the world, including the United States, particularly in Wisconsin, which has similar weather and soil to Korea and northern China and has produced successful crops for a number of years.

How to Use. Peel the fresh ginger and grate into your chai. Although it is available ground as a powder, crystallized, fresh, and dried, as with all spices, fresh provides the best flavor. Buy fresh ginger in small quantities, perhaps one "leg" at a time. To store, wrap it in a paper towel, place in a plastic bag, and refrigerate for best results. Even leaving the roots in a cool dark place, rather than in the refrigerator, tends to age ginger quickly, making it quite fibrous.

Ayurvedic Benefits. Ginger helps stimulate the circulation, promotes sweating, relaxes blood vessels, and is an antiseptic; it's also used as an expectorant and prevents vomiting. A tisane of ginger and boiling water is excellent for the digestion and for anyone suffering from abdominal bloating, flatulence, or car sickness. A warming herb, it helps sufferers during the onset of migraine; a relative of turmeric, it is often mixed with that spice to help in osteoarthritis. It has excellent toxin-digesting qualities for victims of rheumatism and rheumatoid arthritis. It's good for colds, flus, cramps, and laryngitis as well.

The Indian cure-all for a cold is often a combination of ginger, turmeric, and jaggery (dark sugar), boiled in water as a tisane. Other homebrews for colds include cinnamon and ginger mixed in boiled milk and water, commonly called *ubalo,* Hindi for "boiling."

licorice root

(Glycyrrhiza glabra)

Licorice gives a decidedly sweet bite to chai blends that's infinitely more interesting than sugars. It can, however, mask the tastes of other herbs or spices, so add it with a light touch.

How to Use. The licorice herb is cut up and is usually sold in tea bags, which can easily be placed into the brewing water for your tea and removed before drinking. (The candy is processed from the root, plant, and stems with sugar.)

Ayurvedic Benefits. This spice acts as a mild laxative and is excellent for irritated dyspepsia in asthma. As a tonic it is excellent for glandular and adrenal disorders; it has been recommended for coughs, laryngitis, bronchitis, hiccups, and rejuvenating the reproductive system, especially in men. It pacifies *vata* and *pitta,* but overuse will increase *kapha* and cause water retention. It's also known to improve the voice, eyesight, strength, and hair.

nutmeg

(Myristica fragrans)

First brought to Europe from the Banda Islands in 1512 by the Portuguese, nutmeg has a long and colorful history in other parts of the world. Quite likely it was nutmeg that the first-century Roman writer Pliny described as "a tree that produced a nut with two separate flavors." The oval-shaped nutmeg is the hard kernel of an evergreen tree native to the Spice Islands (Moluccas) in Southeast Asia. It is wrapped in a bright red lacy covering called mace or *aril;* both nutmeg and mace are used extensively in Indian cuisine.

For many years Europeans carried nutmeg in graters with a lidded container to hold the kernel so that it could be grated whenever desired. Modern nutmeg graters are still available in a style that holds a kernel or two for convenience. Nutmeg is known as *javitri* in Hindi and as *rou dou kou* in Chinese.

Mace, which seems to combine the spice of pepper with the heat of cinnamon, is actually more subtle than nutmeg itself. A coffee grinder or professional nut grinder is best to grate mace blades.

How to Use. Add nutmeg or mace to your chai only at the last minute rather than cooking it with other spices. Both lose flavor very quickly when heated.

Ayurvedic Benefits. Nutmeg helps stave off nausea, vomiting, and the diarrhea that comes from food poisoning. It can be used as a digestive and to help relax, especially when insomnia is present.

nutmeg

pepper
(Piper nigrum)

This widely popular spice (the United States is the largest single importer) is the berry of a plant native to the equatorial forests of India. This perennial vine takes eight years to reach maturity, but it bears fruit for up to twenty years afterward. Today it grows in Indonesia, Sri Lanka, Madagascar, and Brazil, although berries from the Malabar Coast of India are considered among the finest. Black, white, and green peppercorns are available from the same berry. The black peppercorn is unripe when picked; it's then dried, and is the most pungent. When left to ripen and its skin removed, it becomes the white peppercorn.

How to Use. Grind peppercorns for each use for freshness and pungency to flavor chais.

Ayurvedic Benefits. Pepper's primary benefit is its warming property.

pepper

woman with amphora

Unpasting herself
from the deep
blue of the sky,
she rises
and walks gently
towards me,
bearing
on her head
an earthen jar
containing
the mysteries
of fresh amphora.
Her shadow
stretches
disappearing
into the blue,
then appears
long and elegant,
dreaming
of Giacometti.
Just as she comes
into focus,
she freezes
within
her tall frame
holding the thaw
of her contents,
the perfume
escaping
just enough
to make me
want more.

— SUDEEP SEN

saffron

(Crocus sativus)

Because the red stigmas of the crocus flower are handpicked, saffron is the world's most expensive spice per ounce, although barely a pinch of powder or just one thread is all that is necessary infuse an entire dish or cup of chai with a wonderful fragrance and taste. Saffron is also used to color tea or food in red-to-yellow shades. Desserts made with saffron, from scones to cakes and cookies, offer a delicate balance to any chai drink. It's grown in Kashmir, India, Greece, and Spain. Check your ethnic markets for lower priced sources.

How to Use. For best flavor use saffron threads rather than the cheaper powders; only one or two are necessary to give a dish color and fragrance. Crush the threads and stir into your dish.

Ayurvedic Benefits. Unknown. Excellent as a flavoring.

star anise

(Illicium verum)

Named for its shape, this spice looks like a star or flower with six to nine "points." (It's also known as Chinese anise or, in Farsi, badayan.) The fruit of a native Chinese evergreen tree, it is a slow starter that does not bear fruit until it is six years old, although some trees have been known to proffer fruit for one hundred years. After its yellow flowers bloom, the brown fruit opens into star shapes, with each point containing a shiny brown seed. The essential oil of star anise (anethole) is slightly stronger than but quite similar to anise.

how to grind spices for chai

The spice grinder's best tool remains the mortar and pestle. This stone cup and oblong tool, shaped like a thick baseball bat, requires "elbow grease" but provides the chai lover with coarsely ground spices that really amp up the beverage and add the sparkle of spice to your drink.

A battery-powered or motorized spice grinder is also a great tool, but it's easy to overgrind and the results are powdered spices, which have diffused flavors. Ground spices are best used in baking. A pepper grinder is a perfect way to add whole peppercorns to chais. Avoid grinding spices in a coffee grinder or nut grinder, unless you will be able to clean it thoroughly. Spices are often so strong they will infuse your next grinding of coffee or nuts.

If you have neither mortar and pestle nor spice grinder, do not despair. A large-blade knife like a Chinese cleaver can be used to smash spices into pieces small enough for your chai.

How to Use. Place one star anise pod in a cup and pour in your chai; lovely! Star anise can be used whole (the pods are pretty and really do look like stars), or can be either crushed or ground for a milder taste. The Iranians use star anise in a spice blend known as *dhnajeera*, and Middle Eastern markets are good sources for this special spice. It has a delicate, sweet taste similar to that of anise, the tiny oval seed of the fennel plant *(Foeniculum vulgare)*. For more information on fennel, see page 96.

Ayurvedic Benefits. A diuretic and stimulant, star anise is quite beneficial for sore throats when made into a tisane.

To make, simply pour boiling water over two or three pods in a cup, allow to steep for 3 to 5 minutes, and add sweetener, if desired. Sip slowly.

vanilla

(Vanilla planifolia)

Originally from Mexico, the vanilla bean was used as far back as the time of the Aztecs for flavoring hot chocolate. It was the Aztecs who learned how to cure the beans of this climbing orchid by repeatedly sweating and drying them to develop the white crystalline vanillin. Tahiti and Mexico, particularly the state of Veracruz, produce excellent vanilla, and it is also grown in Madagascar, Puerto Rico, Réunion, and throughout Central America.

How to Use. It's best to use vanilla in its supple dark brown bean state, and though they are expensive, the beans can be used more than once: Split them, scrape out the seeds, and leave the beans to dry for several days. Keeping dried beans in a sealed container of sugar adds the intoxicating aroma of vanilla to the sugar. If you must use vanilla extract, use pure extract; the synthetic has an unpleasant aftertaste that can spoil your chai.

Ayurvedic Benefits. Unknown. Excellent as a flavoring.

vanilla

chai accompaniments

From food are born all creatures which live upon food and after death return to food. Food is the chief of all things. It is therefore said to be the medicine of all diseases of the body.

— THE UPANISHADS, 500 B.C.

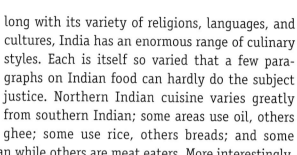

along with its variety of religions, languages, and cultures, India has an enormous range of culinary styles. Each is itself so varied that a few paragraphs on Indian food can hardly do the subject justice. Northern Indian cuisine varies greatly from southern Indian; some areas use oil, others ghee; some use rice, others breads; and some groups are vegetarian while others are meat eaters. More interestingly, each region uses spices most appropriate for its weather, because some spices cool the body and others are warming, thus nurturing the body and the spirit at the same time. This cool versus warm property of spices is one of the principles of ayurvedic medicine.

traditional indian savories (namkiin)

The foods most commonly served with chais are savories, of which there are literally hundreds of variations; I can only describe a few of them here. Chai is the perfect balance for these often quite hot savories made with chilis, heavy doses of garam masala, plus additional spices.

Most savories are not, however, for the calorie or time conscious, because many are deep-fried to be served immediately after cooking. Fortunately, many Indian grocers have frozen interpretations that you can simply thaw and fry at home, a great time saver. Some brands can be heated in the microwave for the best of both worlds — no prep and no frying.

sev

This marvelous snack uses a special tool called a sev *mold that's like a large garlic press. If your local Indian grocer doesn't have one, you can form chunky strips by hand or use a grinder set on large holes to achieve the same shapes, or use a spaetzle press.*

2½ cups gram or *besan* (chickpea) flour

½ teaspoon chili powder

½ teaspoon asafetida (hing)

½ teaspoon ajwain (omum)

Canola oil, as necessary

Salt, to taste

1. Mix the gram or *besan* flour, chili powder, asafetida, ajwain, and a little heated canola oil, about ½ teaspoon. Add enough water to form into a stiff but smooth dough. Knead well.

2. Divide into small portions (about 1-inch) and reserve.

3. Heat about 1 tablespoon of canola oil in a deep frying pan. When a drop of water sizzles when dripped into the oil, you're ready to add the dough.

4. Place a portion of dough in a *sev* mold, hold the mold over the hot oil, and press carefully until the entire dough portion is passed through the sieves at the base of the mold. Let the *sev* fall gently into the hot oil, frying one portion at a time.

5. Using a wooden spoon, move the pieces of *sev* dough in a circular motion. Turn and fry the *sev* till golden and crisp, taking care not to burn them.

6. Drain and place on paper towels or kraft paper. Cool and store in an airtight container.

6 servings

Ingredients

16 whole raw almonds

½ pound lean ground lamb

1 large egg

¼ teaspoon salt

⅛ teaspoon freshly ground black pepper

3 tablespoons gram or *besan* (chickpea) flour

1 tablespoon spring water

1 cup canola oil, for frying

¼ cup ghee (Indian-style clarified butter; see page 114

¼ cup finely chopped onion

½ teaspoon finely chopped garlic

½ tablespoon chopped fresh ginger

koftas

These spicy meatballs are to Indian cuisine what Swedish meatballs are to Scandinavian cuisine, but spicier, more flavorful, and, I think, infinitely more interesting. They go well with rice. This recipe can easily be doubled or tripled.

1. Soak the almonds in boiling water to cover for about 2 hours; drain and discard the water.

2. In a large bowl, combine the lamb, egg, salt, and pepper with 1½ tablespoons of the chickpea flour. Knead with your hands then beat with a wooden spoon until smooth and well integrated.

3. Divide the mixture into eight equal portions. Shape each into a flat round, place an almond in the center, and enclose the meat around the nut until you have a ball shape.

4. In a separate bowl, make a batter with the remaining chickpea flour and the water. Spread the batter evenly on all sides of the meatballs (your fingers are fine) and place them side by side on a piece of wax paper.

5. Using a wok or deep fryer, heat the canola oil to at least 375°F and deep-fry about three or four meatballs at a time, turning them with a slotted spoon over and over until they brown. As each meatball completely browns, transfer it to a plate covered with a paper towel or Kraft paper, to absorb additional oil. Repeat until all the meatballs are cooked.

6. In another pan, heat the ghee until hot; add the onion, garlic, and ginger and cook lightly for about 2 minutes. Add the turmeric, cumin, coriander, and hot pepper and stir constantly

for about 10 minutes or until the onion is golden. Stir in the yogurt, mixing thoroughly.

7. Spoon in the meatballs until they are thoroughly covered with the onion mixture, then sprinkle the garam masala spices over everything. Cover the pan tightly, reduce the heat to low, and simmer for about 10 more minutes.

8. Remove from the heat and let the mixture rest for about 1 hour (do not remove the lid). To serve, simmer gently for just 5 minutes, then pour onto a deep platter and garnish with the fresh coriander.

2 servings

Too small a harvest of onions is tantamount to a crisis in India, for onion is the most frequently used ingredient in cuisines throughout this vast and marvelous country.

¼ **teaspoon ground turmeric**

¼ **teaspoon ground cumin**

¼ **teaspoon ground coriander**

⅛ **teaspoon ground hot pepper, e.g. cayenne**

½ **cup plain yogurt, drained and thickened**

½ **teaspoon garam masala spices (see page 115)**

1 **tablespoon finely chopped fresh coriander (aka cilantro or Chinese parsley)**

PASTRY DOUGH

¾ cup all-purpose white flour

½ teaspoon salt

½ teaspoon unsalted butter, melted

¾ cup milk less 1 tablespoon, warmed but not boiled

Corn or canola oil, for frying

samosas

These scrumptious deep-fried pasties can be filled with vegetables or meat. Every household has its own recipe; here's one to whet your appetite and tempt your culinary skills. These are an ideal way to make a treat from yesterday's leftovers. Flavored chutneys or salsas taste wonderful with them, plus your favorite milky chai.

1. To make the pastry dough, sift the flour and salt into a mixing bowl. Make a well in the middle of the flour and add ½ teaspoon of butter and the milk. Mix well and knead into a stiff dough. Cover with a damp linen cloth and set aside in a warm spot.

2. To make the *samosa* stuffing, melt the 2 tablespoons of butter in a medium size frying pan. Fry the onion until it's cooked but not browned. Add the remaining stuffing ingredients and mix well. Cook, stirring frequently, until the mixture has absorbed the butter and is dry. Remove from the heat and let cool, uncovered.

3. Cut the dough into quarters, and divide each quarter into six parts. Roll each out into a thin round.

4. In the center of each round, place a spoonful of filling. To fold, dampen the edges of the dough with milk and fold into a half circle (like a mini empanada or turnover). Press the edges together, crimping them like the edges of a piecrust. The most popular samosa shape is a pyramid.

5. Heat about a tablespoon of oil in a frying pan until a drop of water spatters, then slowly and carefully lay the *samosas* in the pan with a spatula, turning them several times until golden brown.

chai accompaniments

6. Remove and drain well on Kraft paper or paper towels. Repeat until all of the *samosas* are done. Serve immediately while hot.

Serves 12 people as appetizers,
6 as a part of a meal

Even a small amount of cilantro adds zing to nearly any dish

STUFFING

2 tablespoons (¼ stick) unsalted butter

1 yellow onion, minced fine

1 pound Yukon Gold or small White Rose potatoes, peeled, boiled, and mashed

1½ teaspoons salt, or less to taste

½ teaspoon or more chili powder, to taste

½ teaspoon garam masala spices (see page 115)

1 tablespoon chopped fresh cilantro

2 teaspoons freshly squeezed lemon juice

¾ cup grated fresh cauliflower or broccoli, drained of excess moisture

1 fresh red chili, chopped (Mexican or Indian, as available)

1 large yellow onion, minced

1 teaspoon ground cayenne pepper

1 teaspoon garam masala spice mix (see page 115)

2 teaspoons chili powder

2 teaspoons salt

1 teaspoon ground turmeric

1 tablespoon chopped fresh cilantro

¾ cup all-purpose wheat flour

¾ cup ground rice powder

1 ounce fine semolina

Cold water, about ¼ cup or more as needed

Canola or corn oil, for frying

pakoras

These delicious Indian savories are deep-fried vegetable fritters, rolled with flour to make a fried dumpling rather than stuffed inside a dough covering like samosas. They're spicier, too, with the use of chili powder, cayenne, and fresh chilis. Dried chilis can be substituted for fresh. This is indeed a strong-tasting dish, so feel free to reduce the cayenne to a pinch and the chili powder to perhaps 1 teaspoon.

Pakoras taste delicious with a mango-tomato salsa or a mango chutney. Bottled chutneys are widely available on the condiment shelves of grocery stores. To make a mango salsa, add 1 chopped fresh mango to 1 cup of chunky tomato salsa; mix in about 1 teaspoon of chopped fresh cilantro and salt to taste. The sweetness of the mango cuts the sharpness of the tomatoes, and the "yin-yang" of it all is wonderful with Indian savories. Papayas can be substituted for mangoes.

1. Mix the vegetables, chili, and onion with the spices and dry ingredients. Slowly add enough cold water to form a thick batter.

2. Heat the oil in a pan until a drop of water spatters when dripped into the oil. With a large tablespoon, drop spoonfuls of the batter gently into the hot oil. Flatten each slightly into a small pancake. Fry until golden brown and crisp. Try to turn only once.

3. Remove from the pan and drain well on Kraft paper or paper towels. Repeat until all the pancakes are done. Serve immediately while hot.

Makes about 3 dozen small pancakes, enough for 12 people for appetizers or 6 people as a side dish with a meal, along with your favorite chai

barfi

This Indian "fudge" is available in a light brown or bright green pistachio (pista) flavor, or a dark brown almond (badam) flavor. It's very sugary sweet with a crumbly texture and fudgelike consistency. The following is an almond and pistachio barfi *that is perfect for a chai made without milk or sugar. The spiciness of the tea beautifully balances the sweetness of the* barfi.

1 cup slivered blanched almonds

1 cup unsalted pistachios

4 teaspoons ghee (Indian-style clarified butter; see page 114)

1 quart whole milk

1 cup sugar

½ teaspoon pure almond extract

1. Pulverize the nuts in a grinder or blender until they are a smooth powder. Set aside.

2. Spread about 1 teaspoon of the ghee over a 7½-inch pie tin using a pastry brush or wax paper.

3. Bring the milk to a boil in a heavy saucepan over high heat. Reduce the heat to medium and continue cooking the milk, stirring frequently, until it thickens to the consistency of a heavy cream (about 30 minutes). Slowly pour in the sugar and stir for an additional 10 minutes.

4. Slowly add the nut powder and cook for 10 minutes more, stirring continuously. Add the remaining ghee and cook for about 7 minutes, stirring until thick enough to form a solid mass.

5. Remove from heat and stir in almond extract. Carefully pour the mixture into the pie tin, smoothing it with a rubber spatula.

6. Allow to cool for about 30 minutes. Cut the *barfi* into triangles or diamonds at this point, because it will harden as it cools further and will become difficult to cut.

24 pieces

carrot halwa

3 medium carrots (about ½ pound), scraped and coarsely grated

1 quart whole milk

½ cup light cream

½ cup dark brown sugar, packed, mixed with 1 teaspoon dark molasses

¼ cup granulated sugar

¾ cup whole blanched unsalted almonds, pulverized in a grinder or blender

2 tablespoons ghee (Indian-style clarified butter; see page 114)

½ teaspoon cardamom seeds, crushed

2 tablespoons unsalted roasted pistachio nuts

2 tablespoons unsalted, slivered, blanched almonds, toasted

A favorite of the Sikhs of Punjab, carrot halwa *originated from nut dishes introduced by traders from the Middle East and Asia Minor during the Moghul period. Indians have used a variety of vegetables for* halwa, *including pumpkins, zucchinis and other squashes, potatoes and yams, and even winter melons. Some recipes substitute ricotta cheese and dry milk for the whole milk used here, but I believe fresh milk produces a richer and smoother sweet. Halwa can be kept refrigerated for several days, then heated prior to serving.*

1. In a heavy saucepan, combine the carrots, milk, and cream and bring to a boil over high heat, stirring continuously.

2. Reduce the heat to moderate and cook for 1 hour, stirring frequently, until the mixture has been reduced by half and coats a wooden spoon thickly.

3. Stir in the brown sugar, molasses, and granulated sugar and cook for 10 minutes. Reduce the heat to its lowest setting, add the ground almonds and ghee, and stir for 10 more minutes or until thick enough to form a heavy mass.

4. Remove from the heat and stir in the cardamom seeds. Spread the *halwa* on a heatproof platter and decorate with pistachios and slivered almonds. Serve at room temperature, or warm.

4 servings

jalebis

These are Indian doughnuts, crisp, deep-fried batter immersed in a rose water-infused syrup. Prepare the batter the day before, because it must rest for 12 hours.

1. Combine the warm water, baking powder, rice flour, and all-purpose flour into a smooth batter. Allow the batter to rest at room temperature, uncovered, for 12 hours or overnight.

2. When the batter has finished resting, combine the sugar, cold water, and cream of tartar in a deep saucepan and stir over moderate heat until the sugar dissolves. Increase the heat to high. Bring the mixture to a boil then let it cook, undisturbed, for 5 additional minutes. Its temperature should reach 220°F on a candy thermometer.

3. Remove from the heat and stir in the food colorings and rose water. Pour the syrup into a bowl and set aside.

4. Pour the canola oil into a deep fryer or large wok and heat to 350°F. The tricky part is shaping the *jalebis*. Use a pastry bag filled with about 1 cup of batter at a time, and squeeze it directly into the hot oil, drawing lines back and forth several times to form a pretzel of figure-eights or lines; the shapes are certainly up to your creative bent, but each *jalebi* should be about 2 by 3 inches if it's to fry quickly and easily. Fry four or five *jalebis* at a time for 2 minutes or until golden on both sides. When done, transfer to the syrup to coat for a minute, then transfer to a warm plate. Repeat until all the batter is cooked.

60 jalebis

2 cups lukewarm water (110–115°F)

¼ teaspoon double-acting baking powder

¼ cup rice flour

3 cups all-purpose white flour

4 cups sugar

3 cups cold water

⅛ teaspoon cream of tartar

2 teaspoons yellow food coloring

⅛ teaspoon red food coloring

1 teaspoon rose water

3 cups canola oil

classic indian condiments

The cuisine of India is as complex, as exciting, as varied as its languages, religions, and people. There are, however, a few foods that are used in nearly every region. The first is a combination of spices called garam masala. A clarified butter known as ghee is used extensively as are onions by the bushelful. What follows are "must-use" condiments every Indian cook must learn to make.

1 pound unsalted butter

ghee

This Indian-style clarified butter is an oil made by cooking butter long enough to clear it of its fat and enhance its flavor to an almost nutty taste. Simple clarified butter is not the same thing.

1. Melt butter in a heavy saucepan over moderate heat without letting it brown.

2. Increase the heat and bring the butter to a boil until its surface is covered with white foam.

3. Reduce the heat and simmer, uncovered, for about 45 minutes, or until the milk solids on the bottom are a golden brown and the butter on top is transparent.

4. Remove from the heat and pour through a fine sieve or dampened cheesecloth into a large bowl. Re-strain as often as necessary; even tiny pieces of solids will turn the ghee rancid.

5. Pour the perfectly clear ghee into a jar, cover tightly, and store in the refrigerator. Simply reheat over a low flame.

1½ cups

garam masala

This blend of spices is typical of a dry masala used in cooking. By adding coconut or other "wet" ingredients, you can achieve a wet masala. With variations, this mixture can be used to make Indian spice tea or milky chai, or added to any food item in which you want the taste of chai. The amounts here are on the spicy side, so adjust according to your taste. This blend will keep for months in a jar with a tight lid, stored in a cool, dark cupboard.

1 cup whole green cardamom pods

½ cup whole cloves

½ cup whole cumin seeds

½ cup whole black peppercorns

¼ cup whole coriander seeds

5 3-inch pieces of cinnamon stick

1. Preheat the oven to 200°F.

2. In a large, shallow roasting pan, spread a layer of the spices. Roast them in the oven for about 30 minutes, avoid over-browning or burning.

3. Remove the pan from the oven and allow the seeds to cool. Open each cardamom pod, pull the pod from the seeds, and discard. Set the seeds aside. When cool, immediately pour into a jar, tighten the lid securely, and store in a cool, dark place.

4. Crush the cinnamon sticks by placing them between the folds of a plain-weave cotton towel and pounding with a meat mallet or rolling pin until finely crushed. A mortar and pestle can be used.

5. Combine all the spices until thoroughly mixed.

6. Grind the spices in an electric grinder or blender until they reach the consistency of a powder.

1¼ cups

paneer

1 quart whole milk

1 tablespoon fresh lemon juice

This is the most popular form of Indian cheese: soft, creamy, made with a whole milk that makes it just the right consistency for sweet dishes. Paneer is excellent with fruit or chai-flavored pastries like the scones on page 52 or with plain cookies. It can be refrigerated for up to two weeks between uses.

1. In a large saucepan, bring the milk to a boil over medium heat.
2. Remove the pan from the heat and add the lemon juice. Stir well until the curds and whey separate from each other.
3. Pour the entire contents of the saucepan through a piece of cheesecloth. Tie the cloth and squeeze out as much liquid as possible. If using a sieve, push a spatula onto the cheese until the liquid seeps out. Allow the cheese to continue to drain for at least 1 hour.

4 cups

The tanginess of fresh lemon juice gives *paneer* unique bite.

chai ros malai
quick "indian" cream

This recipe from Chef Robert Wemischner is a delicious alternative to the Indian paneer that is the basis for many Indian desserts. Paneer is very time consuming to prepare, but this version takes a shortcut by using ricotta cheese. Here chai masala, augmented by some extra sweet spice, goes beyond the china cup to lend its haunting fragrance to the sauce for this dreamy cream.

1. Place the ricotta in a fine sieve set over a bowl to remove excess moisture. Refrigerate overnight, covered.

2. Make the creamy sauce by bringing the milk, sugar, spices, and chai masala to a boil in a medium saucepan. Cook, stirring frequently and deeply into the bottom of the pan, until the mixture has reduced enough to coat the back of a wooden spoon.

3. Remove the pan from the heat and pour the mixture through a fine sieve to remove its solids. Pour into a bowl and let cool. Refrigerate, covered, until cold.

4. To serve, pour a small amount of the sauce on each plate. Using two large soup spoons dipped in hot water, form the ricotta into oval-shaped portions. Center one ricotta oval on each plate and mask thoroughly with the remaining sauce.

6 servings

1 pound ricotta cheese from whole or skim milk

4 cups whole milk

½ cup sugar

5 whole cardamom pods

1 cinnamon stick

4 whole cloves

2 tablespoons chai masala (or dry chai tea mix)

A Traveler's Tale

Our Journey Ends . . . or Does it?

Kashmiri Tea

The air was unexpectedly hot, thick, unmoving — so unlike the familiar cool here in Sausalito, California. I sat for what seemed eons at the bus stop, my mind floating on waves of heat, when a little white car rolled in front of me. Thinking the driver wanted directions, I got up. A gentleman leaned over and asked in a heavy Indian accent if I was going to San Rafael.

"Come, I take you, it's very hot today," he said, the matter already settled in his mind.

My skirt and blouse seemed like velvet drapes, drenching me in sweat, next to the airy dance of his thin white clothing. The wind blew in through his window, inflating his gauze shirt and pants like billowing sheets hung out to dry. They were whiter than white against the darkness of his skin.

We chatted a few minutes about where he worked and where he lived. Then he asked what I did.

"I write," I said.

"What do you write about?"

"Tea. Chai. I'm a *chaiwallah*."

He smiled again and said, "Ah, *chaiwallah*, yes, you know about this," his accent belying the ten years he had lived here. "Yes, oh yes, chai. I make very good Kashmiri chai, have you ever had this?"

With expansive hand gestures and great flourish, he revealed his own method: boiling the tea for at least an hour and a half, pouring hot water over the leaves many times during the cooking process, adding spices in just the right amount. "Time is very important, because the leaves are very big, the tea is, how you say?" he asked, tugging at my little finger. "Like this, very . . ."

"Thick? Hardy?" I asked.

"Yes, so that is why we cook it for such a long time, pouring water on it again and again. Many times you must do it so that it is just right. It is very good, my chai; it is a pleasure to drink all day long. In my country, we have every morning this chai. Special street vendors," he started to explain.

"*Chaiwallahs,*" we said together. He turned and smiled, laughing lightly. "Yes, you know this very well. In my country," he went on, "the *chaiwallahs,* they get up very early in the morning to make good chai for everyone to drink all day long."

"Do you cook?" I asked.

Throughout the day, every day, everyone in India stops for tea to warm or cool them as desired, and to enjoy the national beverage of choice.

"Yes. I'm a very good cook," he said, lifting up his chin with pride. "Every time I cook, all the neighbors come by and ask, 'What is that wonderful smell? What are you cooking?' It is not hard, this cooking, but it takes much time."

The cars beside us became a kaleidoscope of colors as he sped along, telling me how Indian dancers and musicians had entertained at the recent street fair in San Rafael. "Americans, they seem to like Indian music; I don't know why. But they come every time to the fair to hear our music."

"Do you play an instrument, are you a musician, too?" I asked.

"No, but I sing very well. Here, listen." His pointed index finger signaled some unspoken downbeat. "I will show you." He sat up with his back ramrod straight in his driver's seat, his head facing forward more assuredly. His light baritone voice poured out a lilting Indian song. It went on for several choruses, ending when he turned and smiled as if to say, "It is true, I sing very well, yes?"

"Very lovely," I said. I was about to ask him more when he tapped his forefinger on my hand and said, "Wait, wait, I'll sing you another. Listen careful now," like a father rewarding a child for good behavior. As he swayed his head from side to side, from out of his smiling lips came a haunting melody.

Touched by the sweetness, I whispered, "What does it mean, this song?"

He smiled knowingly. "Love is like a paper boat," he explained. "Love is like a paper boat." He moved his hands through the air in impersonation of a gliding boat. "It floats along the water, sometimes with the wind, and sometimes it sinks, because love is like a paper boat."

He smiled again, showing his perfectly white teeth, the front ones considerably longer than the side, his smile beatific. He slowed down to a stop and said, "I'll let you out here," ending my reverie as abruptly as it began.

I hummed his melody all the way to work, unable to let it slip away. Tonight the melody returns to me, and for the first time, when the wind howls and rocks my floating home on the bay, my fears abate as the spicy aroma of Kashmiri chai wafts through my window.

India's remarkable tolerance for variety is reflected in the many magnificent temples, mosques, churches, and synagogues placed throughout the country.

recommended reading

Evans, Charles M., with Roberta Lee Pliner. *The Terrarium Book*. New York: Random House, 1973.

Fletcher, David Wilson. *Himalayan Tea Garden*. New York: Thomas Y. Crowell, 1955.

Fortune, Robert. *A Residence Among the Chinese: Inland, on the Coast and at Sea*. 1857. Reprint, Wilmington, Del.: Scholarly Resources, Inc., 1972.

———. *Three Years' Wanderings in the Northern Provinces of China, Including a Visit to the Tea, Silk, and Cotton Countries*. 2d ed. London: John Murray, 1847.

———. *Two Visits to the Tea Countries of China and the British Tea Plantations in the Himalayas*, vol. 2. 3rd ed. London: John Murray, 1853.

———. *Yedo and Peking: A Narrative of a Journey to the Capitals of Japan and China*. London: John Murray, 1863.

Lad, Vasant. *Ayurveda: The Science of Self-Healing*. Twin Lakes, WI Lotus Light Publications, 1985.

Maitland, Derek. *5000 Years of Tea: A Pictorial Companion*. Recipes by Jacki Passmore. New York: Gallery Books, an imprint of W. H. Smith Publishers, Inc., 1982.

Ody, Penelope. *The Complete Medicinal Herbal*. London: Dorling Kindersley, Inc., 1993.

Ortiz, Elisabeth Lambert. *The Encyclopedia of Herbs, Spices & Flavorings*. London: Dorling Kindersley, Inc., 1992.

Stella, Alain, Gilles Brochard, Nadine Beautheae, and Catherine Donzel. *The Book of Tea*. With a foreword by Anthony Burgess. Paris, France: Flammarion, 1992; distributed in U.S. by Abbeville Press.

Svoboda, Robert E. *Prakruti: Your Ayurvedic Constitution*. Albuquerque: Geocom, 1989.

Ukers, William H. *All About Tea*. 2 vols. 1935. Reprint, Westport, Conn.: Hyperion Press, 1994.

Zabarkes, Adriana, and Rochelle Zabarkes. *Adriana's Spice Caravan: Cooking with Spices, Rubs, and Blends from Around the World*. Pownal, VT: Storey Publishing, 1997.

glossary

Many ingredients are commonly used in masala chai and in Indian cookery, and many words are used to describe the experience of drinking chai. The following glossary should help you in your journey through the world of chai.

But first, a note on the languages you'll find here: India is a country of many, many tongues, including Tamil, Assam, Bangalore, Goa, Gujarati, Punjabi, Telugu, Marathi, Urdu, and Nepali, plus the three most used in describing food: Bengali, Hindi, and Kashmiri. It is not unusual for words of one language to overlap into another, so I have opted for the phrase "generic Indian word" to describe such universal usage. These are words that everyone in India knows, whether they speak Punjabi or Urdu or anything in between. These are also the words used in most Indian spice shops and groceries here in the United States; when you want to order Indian items for yourself, these words will be clearly understood.

Sanskrit is the language used to describe aspects of the Ayurvedic system of health care so widely applied throughout India. I have retained these words as they are used by Ayurvedic practitioners throughout the world.

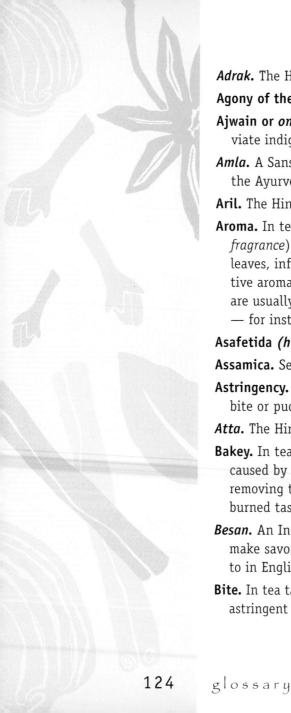

Adrak. The Hindi word for "ginger."

Agony of the leaves. The unfolding of tea leaves in boiling water.

Ajwain or *omum (Carum copticuma).* Wild caraway, used to alleviate indigestion, colic, or internal gas.

Amla. A Sanskrit word referring to one of the six basic tastes in the Ayurvedic system, defined as "sour."

Aril. The Hindi word for mace.

Aroma. In tea tasting, this term (or the similar *nose* and *fragrance*) refers to the scent of a tea's innate character. Dry leaves, infused leaves, and the tea liquor itself all have distinctive aromas peculiar to their region, and even to estate. Aromas are usually described by making analogies with flowers or fruits — for instance, an oolong's aroma may be said to be peachlike.

Asafetida *(hing).* A popular Indian spice.

Assamica. See *Camellia sinensis* var. *assamica.*

Astringency. In tea tasting, this term refers to a flavor quality of bite or puckeriness in the liquor.

Atta. The Hindi word for flour.

Bakey. In tea tasting, this term refers to an unpleasant taste caused by firing tea leaves at too high a temperature and thus removing too much moisture. A bakey taste is not as strong as a burned taste.

Besan. An Indian word for the chickpea flour commonly used to make savory snacks to be eaten with masala chai. Often referred to in English as gram flour.

Bite. In tea tasting, this term refers not to a taste, but to the astringent puckeriness that gives black tea its refreshing quality.

Black. In tea tasting, this term refers to the dark brownish black appearance of the fully dried leaf.

Bloom. In tea tasting, this term refers to sheen that results from careful handling, sorting, and manufacture of the tea leaves.

Body. In tea tasting, this term refers to viscosity, to the strength of the liquor combined with its weight on the tongue. Body may be "full," "light," and so forth.

Bright. In tea tasting, this term refers to a "bright" appearance in the tea leaf, or to a lively, sparkling taste in the tea liquor (the opposite of a dull taste).

Brisk. In tea tasting, this term refers to a flavor characteristic of liveliness, or a light, pleasurably dry taste in the mouth.

Camellia sinensis. The botanical name for the tea bush, an evergreen shrub that grows to great heights and in thirty-five different countries; India is the largest producer of teas in the entire world.

***Camellia sinensis* var. *assamica*.** A variety of wild tea plant indigenous to the Assam region of India.

Cardamom. A seed used as a spice that comes from a pod. Unroasted cardamom seeds are green, and roasted are black. They add a smoky, soft taste to foods and beverages. In Indian stores, the spice is referred to as *ilaichi* or *elaichi* for green cardamom and *chhoti ilaichi* for black cardamom.

Chai. The Hindi word for tea. Many variations of the spelling, from *cha* to *tcha* to *tay,* have filtered down from the original Chinese *cha* to the English *tea,* referring to the beverage made from the leaves of the *Camellia sinensis.*

Chai latte. An American phrase that combines the Hindi word *chai* and the Italian word *latte,* to describe a drink of steamed milk made with chai spices, although the word *latte* is more commonly used to refer to a milky drink made with coffee.

Chaiwallah (chayvalas). The Hindi word for a vendor *(wallah)* who sells tea *(chai),* most typically in railroad stations throughout northern India.

Channa. The Hindi word for chickpea.

Chevdo (chudra). The generic Indian word for the snack typically eaten with masala chai, a mélange of sharp spices, raisins, peanuts, and fried rice puffs. It's also made with corn puffs.

Chini (cheene). The generic Indian word for sugar.

Clean. In tea tasting, this term refers to a tea leaf free of fiber, dust, twigs, or similar particles.

Coppery. In tea tasting, this term refers to well-processed tea leaves that have a reddish overcast.

Creaming up. In tea tasting, this term refers to the bubbly residue that occasionally comes to the surface of black teas, especially Assams. It is harmless, and indeed desirable.

CTC (crush, tear, curl). A method of processing black teas in which the leaves are broken and made into the stronger tasting, higher caffeine dark teas typically found in tea bags. CTC is not necessarily a low-grade tea, but it does generally provide a darker and more intensely flavored beverage in the cup than the more delicate whole-leaf teas, whether they're processed green, oolong, or black.

Dalchini. The generic Indian word for cinnamon.

Dark. In tea tasting, this term refers to a dull or dark color in tea leaves, indicating poor quality.

Dhania. The generic Indian word for coriander.

Doodh. The generic Indian word for milk.

Doshas. The Sanskrit word used to describe the three humors or waste products of digestion cited in the Ayurvedic system of health. These three humors are known as *kapha* (water or phlegm), *pitta* (fire or bile), and *vata* (air or wind). *Kapha, pitta,* and *vata* are also Sanskrit words.

Flat. In tea tasting, this term refers to a soft, rather flabby-bodied tea that lacks bite and briskness, or to a dull, old taste that indicates a lack of freshness.

Fruity. In tea tasting, this term refers to a piquant flavor (characteristic of Nilgiris, for example) that is redolent of fruity scents.

Garam masala. A specific mixture of spices. This can be used either in cooking or in spice tea. The recipes are infinite.

Ghari (khurrie). A generic Indian word (literally "made with mud") used to refer to the little clay chai-filled cups offered by *chai-wallahs* at train stations. The cups are thrown away when the tea has been drunk, making this an economical and hygienic way of serving tea to the masses.

Ghee. A generic Indian word used to refer to a style of clarified butter that's used extensively in various cuisines throughout India.

Gone off. In tea tasting, this term refers to tea that has been spoiled by improper storage or packing, or is simply past its prime and stale. If your merchant tries to sell you this, go to another merchant. Quickly.

Goodh or *gur* **(jaggery).** The generic Indian words used to describe unrefined lump sugar made from the juice of sugarcane or palm sap that is boiled until thick, poured into molds, and allowed to dry into a lumpy mass. It adds a distinctive dark brown sugar taste to chai.

Gram. An English word for the chickpea flour that is used in Indian cuisine, especially in savory snacks. The Hindi words are *channa* (chickpea) and *atta* (flour).

Harsh. In tea tasting, this term refers to a rough taste that results from underwithering and careless manufacture.

High fired. In tea tasting, this term refers to a leaf that has been overfired but not to the point of becoming burned or off tasting. It is sometimes acceptable, but hardly the premier tea sought by connoisseurs.

Javitri. The generic Indian word for nutmeg.

Kapha. The Sanskrit word for one of the three *doshas* of the Ayurvedic system of health. *Kapha* governs water or phlegm.

Kasaya. A Sanskrit word referring to one of the six basic tastes in the Ayurvedic system, defined as "astringent."

Katur. A Sanskrit word referring to one of the six basic tastes in the Ayurvedic system, defined as "pungent."

Khakhra. Roasted wheat-flour chips eaten as snacks in India. *Methi* is made with red peppers and bitter greens; *masala* chips are made with red peppers; plain *khakhra* are lightly seasoned wheat chips.

Khir. An Indian word for pudding, usually made with rice and milk.

Lavana. A Sanskrit word referring to one of the six basic tastes in the Ayurvedic system, defined as "salty."

Leafy. In tea tasting, this term refers to those teas whose leaves are large or long.

Luong. The generic Indian word for clove; it may come from the Nepali language.

Madhura. A Sanskrit word referring to one of the six basic tastes in the Ayurvedic system, defined as "sweet."

Malty. In tea tasting, this term refers to a subtle underlying flavor. It's often characteristic of Assam teas.

Masala. A generic Indian word for any spice blend, but used in this book to refer to a spice blend for tea that includes some or all of the following: cloves, ginger, pepper, cinnamon, and cardamom.

Masala chai. The generic Indian phrase used to describe an Indian tea drink made with spices, or with spices and milk.

Maza. The generic Indian word for "great fun."

Mazedar **chai.** The generic Indian phrase for "tea that is fun to drink," now archaic and rarely used. *Mazedar* is an adjective that means "fun."

Muscatel. In tea tasting, this term refers to a grapy or winy taste characteristic of Darjeeling teas. Jungpana is the most sought-after "muscatel" Darjeeling.

Musty. In tea tasting, this term refers to a moldy smell that results from poor storage or packing. If you smell mustiness in any tea except a pu-erh, run to another merchant. Pu-erhs, however, are supposed to smell musty, even moldy, which reflects the "friendly" bacteria inherent in them.

Mutkah. The Hindi word for "mud." The term is sometimes used in Bombay to refer to a clay pitcher.

Namkiin. The generic Indian word used to describe spicy, crunchy snacks made in hundreds and hundreds of styles, but generally with gram or *besan* (chickpea) or wheat flour, and sometimes with cashews or peanuts. They are frequently fried or roasted. Their tang and spiciness go well with creamy, frothy chai drinks.

Nan. A spicy or plain fried bread, thin and crisp, common in Indian cuisine; its shape resembles that of a tortilla, but incorporates Indian spices and wheat flour.

Neat. A grade of tea with good-size leaves and fine workmanship.

Nose. See aroma.

Pai cha. The Chinese phrase for "white tea." Still a rarity in India, white tea requires plucking only the tender buds of the tea bush and lightly withering them; no oxidation takes place at all.

Papdi gathiya. Chips made from gram or *besan* (chickpea) flour and shaped into wavy pieces. These snacks are typically eaten with spicy masala chai and are hugely popular throughout India.

Peak. In tea tasting, this term refers to the high point of the tasting experience when, some instants after the liquor enters your mouth, its body, flavor, and astringency make themselves fully felt. Greens and oolongs do not peak, but stand immediately and fully revealed.

Pitta. The Sanskrit word for one of the three humors of the Ayurvedic system of health. *Pitta* governs fire or bile.

Powdery. In tea tasting, this term refers to a fine, light tea dust.

Ragged. In tea tasting, this term refers to badly manufactured tea that is uneven.

Rou dou kou. The Chinese phrase for nutmeg.

Self-drinking. In tea tasting, this term refers to any tea with sufficient aroma, flavor, body, and color to stand alone and in no need of blending for improvement.

Sev. Perhaps the best-known snack throughout India, made from *besan* or gram flour.

Shahad. The Hindi word for honey.

Shakkar. The Hindi word for sugar.

Soft. In tea tasting, this term refers to a flavor quality that is the opposite of brisk. Inefficient firing causes this lack of liveliness and flat taste.

Sonf. A Hindi word for aniseed.

Sonth. A Hindi word for dried ginger.

Stalk and fiber. These plant residues are generally included in lower-grade teas but should be at a minimum in higher grades. They reflect sloppy or indifferent sorting.

Stewed. In tea tasting, this term refers to oversteeped tea leaves that have turned bitter; it can also refer to leaves that have been poorly fired at low temperatures and with insufficient airflow, resulting in a brew with a bitter taste.

Tarry. In tea tasting, this term refers to a smoky aroma (found in Lapsang Souchong or some Russian Caravan–style teas, for instance) that derives from being smoked over wood or charcoal.

Thick. In tea tasting, this term refers to a brew with rich color, taste, and strength.

Thin. In tea tasting, this term refers to a tea that lacks body and/or color; one that tastes more watery than flavorful.

Tip. Literally, the tip of the youngest tea leaves. The presence of tips on tea leaves is a sign of good picking. Tip can appear to be golden or silvery.

Tippy. In tea tasting, this term refers to tea leaves that have a generous amount of silvery or golden tip, or budding leaf.

Tisane. An herbal infusion, usually made with flowers, weeds, or herbs. A chamomile "tea" is therefore not a tea, but an herbal infusion or tisane.

Titka. A Sanskrit word referring to one of the six basic tastes in the Ayurvedic system, defined as "bitter."

Vata. The Sanskrit word for one of the three humors of the Ayurvedic system of health. *Vata* governs air or wind.

Well twisted. In tea tasting, this term refers to fully withered tea leaf that has been tightly rolled lengthwise.

Winy. In tea tasting, this term usually refers to a mellow quality that fine Darjeelings (or Keemuns) acquire with six months to a year or more of aging. More rarely, the term is used as a negative descriptive for overdried tea.

Wiry. In tea tasting, this term refers to stylish, thin whole tea leaves, quite often O.P. (orange pekoe) grade.

Portrait of a Lady

Objects are lessons; from bowls, hairpins, brooches,
you learn of forgotten lives. The stories say
my grandmother was a fever tree;
two birds sat on her branches, one pecking
at a grape, the other singing an aria.

What history's bookkeepers do not show
is the tremor down the spine she felt,
the tendril of blood that coiled in her nose
when the whistle of a train announced
her husband's return from a tour of duty.

In the stories, she's an actor, a pilgrim;
shadow-boxing with a thunderstorm,
she slips through scrubbed floors
and ember beds. She leaves me
a loaf of shortbread in the oven,

a page of couplets in a script I cannot read
and wrapped in a peel of green appleskin,
a tea cup glazed with a Dutch windmill,
the last one of the set.
The urchin-cut waif in the vignette above

is the child she was. Voyeur, clairvoyante, [sic]
she stares in at windows, her head a gourd
hollowed by the age she ever reached
in life, her hair a silver floss.
Objects are lessons; the light seeps
through the slats, sets off a shimmer
on her lace. She's crocheted the evening
and its creatures: the silken thread
that she pulls from her pattern
knots tight around my neck.

— RANJIT HOSKOTE

resources

More and more general supermarkets are devoting space to the spices and foodstuffs of various cultures, to which I shout *hooray*! Obviously, those communities in the United States that have higher concentrations of Indian immigrants will also have more Indian grocery shops. If you don't live near such a community, however, the following sources are a great way to receive spices or Indian specialties via next-day or three-day shipping services. You can order by e-mail and online, by phone, fax, or, should you be so inclined, by "snail mail."

As I have noted throughout this book in both recipes and text, whole spices offer the chai maker fresher taste. Grinding them fresh is critical to capturing the essence of masala chai's drama. I can't imagine anything more wonderful than a slice of fresh ginger in tea; ground ginger is so, well, blah. Crushing some cardamom pods or even adding just a few whole to a plain pot of tea can do more for all your senses than 2 tablespoons of ground spice. Give yourself the gift of good-quality spices. They'll repay you thousandfold.

commercial spice and indian food dealers

ADRIANA'S CARAVAN
409 Vanderbilt Street
Brooklyn, NY 11218
(800) 316-0820 or (718) 436-8565
Fax: (718) 436-8565
e-mail: Adriana@aol.com
Free mail-order catalog of more than fifteen hundred spices, condiments, and exotic ingredients from around the world.

APHRODISIA
264 Bleecker Street
New York, NY 10014
(212) 989-6440
Fax: (212) 989-8027
Offers five different masala spice blends, pre-blended rooibos chais, and a variety of fresh herbs and spices in bulk amounts. Ask for catalog list. Mail order available.

ATLANTIC SPICE COMPANY
PO Box 205
North Truro, MA 02652
(800) 316-7965 or (508) 487-6100
Fax: (508) 487-2550
Web site: www.atlanticspice.com
Source of both whole and powdered spices, including a garam masala mix, plain and blended teas.

CARAVANSERAI
144 East Arques
Sunnyvale, CA 94086
(415) 255-8444
web site: www.caravanserai.com
e-mail: orders@caravanserai.net
Two masala blends: Taj Masala, a classic Moghul masala with cardamom, black pepper, cinnamon, and cloves (unroasted); and Delhi Durbar Garam Masala, a robust, spicier blend with spices roasted whole before mixing. Other Indian spices and teas.

DEAN & DELUCA
560 Broadway
New York, NY 10012
(800) 221-7714 or (212) 431-1619
Free mail-order catalog for fine teas and spices. Seven other locations throughout New York City and in Georgetown: 3276 M Street N.W., Washington, DC 20007; (202) 628-8155.

FRONTIER COOPERATIVE HERBS
PO Box 299
Norway, IA 53218
(800) 669-3275
Web site: www.frontiercoop.com
e-mail: peggy.amans@frontiercoop.com
Extensive free catalog of herbs and spices to scent your chais.

KALUSTYAN
123 Lexington Avenue
New York, NY 10016
(212) 685-3451
International grocer with fine Indian spices and food products.

NATURE'S HERBS
1010 46th Street
Emeryville, CA 94608
(510) 601-0700
Free catalog with an extensive list of spices and herbs, plus their loose rooibos, suitable for herbal chais.

PENZEYS, LTD.
PO Box 1448
Waukesha, WI 53187
(414) 574-0277
The chef's favorite, a family-owned spice firm for whole spices and custom blends of masalas and other combinations.

RAFAL SPICE COMPANY
2521 Russell Street
Detroit, MI 48207
(800) 228-4276 or (313) 259-6373
Fresh spices and spice blends are a specialty.

SAN FRANCISCO HERB COMPANY
250 Fourteenth Street
San Francisco, CA 94103
(800) 227-4530 or (415) 861-7174
Fax: (415) 861-4440
Web site: www.sfherb.com
Excellent source of both whole and powdered spices, including a garam masala mix, plain and blended teas.

SUKHADIA'S SWEETS & SNACKS

Three Locations:
1677 Oak Tree Road
Edison, NJ 08820
(732) 548-1888
Fax: (732) 548-2199
and
661 Route 27
Iselin, NJ 08830
(732) 283-1666
Fax: (732) 283-3233
and
2559 West Devon Avenue
Chicago, IL 60659
(773) 338-5400
Web site: www.sukhadia.com
This food shop has served Indian-cuisine lovers here in the United States for more than ten years. Snacks include bhakervadi, lilo, chevdo, *and* ganthia; *sweets include* badam pista *and* anjeer *rolls,* ghari, pista, *and other favorites.*

SURATI FARSAN MART

11814 East 186th Street
Artesia, CA 90701
(562) 860-2310
Fax: (562) 809-3085
Web site: www.suratifarsan.com
e-mail: info@suratifarsan.com
This market offers a variety of Indian snacks and sweets, plus a dine-in menu and drinks. No matter where you live, you can order online or by e-mail and your barfi *or* puri *will be on its way. All items available by the partial or whole pound.*

VANN'S SPICES

1238 East Joppa Road
Baltimore, MD 21286
(410) 583-1643
An excellent assortment of fine spices.

commercial chai dealers

Chai manufacturers are blending up new recipes every day, so of course this list will never be complete. The following companies, however, have either proved popular for a number of years, or offer exceptional products. Many of these chais are ready-made, powdered mixes that are convenient to use, especially when you want to make a chai quickly. Just add hot water and you'll have a frothy, milky, sweet chai.

If you prefer a simple spice tea, with or without milk, consider loose-leaf tea-and-spice blends; these have more of a "tea taste," and you can add milk and/or sweeteners to suit your palate. If you add your own spices, grind them prior to each serving for the most delicious, and beneficial, results. You can add regular or powdered milk, soy or rice milk, and any type of sweetener you prefer: sugar, honey, molasses, maple syrup, or flavored syrups. As I mentioned earlier, it is better to leave out the sweetener than to use an artificial sweetener, because these tend to make chai bitter.

The better the tea, the better the chai. I encourage you to experiment with your own recipes. Like all foods, masala chais are best when made from scratch.

BIG TRAIN CHAI TEA
30052 Aventura, Suite A
Rancho Santa Margarita, CA 92688
(800) Big Train
Web site: www.ChaiTea.com
Spiced Chai, Raspberry Chai, and Orange Chai powdered mixes only need water and can be made hot or cold. Available in vivid purple resealable bags of 12 ounces; each makes ten large mugfuls.

BLUE WILLOW TEA COMPANY: SEE SEATTLE CHAI

CAFFE D'AMORE, INC.
1633 East Walnut Street
PO Box 61180
Pasadena, CA 91106
(800) 999-0171
Web site: www.caffedamore.com
e-mail: PCOMI@caffedamore.com
Powdered mixes in a choice of Chai D'Amore brand of instant spiced and fruit chai lattes in eight black and green tea flavors including Tahitian Vanilla, East India Spice, Forbidden Fruit, Mandarin Orange, and Green Tea with mango, peach, jasmine, and key lime. Available in 12-ounce bags at specialty food stores and coffee shops. Food-service rates available.

CAPPUCINE: SEE CHAI LATTE TEA

CARAVANSERAI
144 East Arques
Sunnyvale, CA 94086
(415) 255-8444
Web site: www.caravanserai.net
e-mail: orders@caravanserai.net
Darjeeling Delight Masala Chai Sachets in a special blend of Darjeeling from the Tongsong Estate. Each sachet has enough whole spices and tea for a four-cup pot of tea. Eight sachets per package. Drink with or without milk.

CELESTIAL SEASONINGS: SEE MOUNTAIN CHAI

CHADO CHAI

8422½ West Third Street
Los Angeles, CA 90048
(213) 655-2056
Fax: (213) 722-6368
e-mail: Chado@aol.com
Authentic chais in easy-to-use tea bags that are larger than most (3 grams) in packages of twenty. Herbal chai is made with rooibos, (African red bush), and Reena's chai and Chado Chai are authentic chais made with pure Assam tea. Both are flavored with spices and easy to make on the stove top; just add milk and sweeteners to taste. Wholesale bulk orders: (213) 722-9438.

CHAI BREWERS

2131 Delaware Avenue
Santa Cruz, CA 95060
(831) 429-8122
Fax: (831) 429-8161
e-mail: sunchai@cruzio.com
A liquid concentrate sold in restaurants and coffee bars. Try regular Masala Chai, Decaf Masala Chai, Ginseng Masala Chai, Male Tonic AphroTEAsiac Chai, Female Tonic AphroTEAsiac Chai, and Chai-a-lai! Iced Chai Latte Concentrate, all using either Ceylon Supreme teas or water-process decaffeinated black teas.

THE CHAI GUY

170 Newton Street
Seattle, WA 98109
(206) 281-8237
e-mail: be159@scn.org
A concentrate with fresh spices sold by mail order in 32-ounce bottles. Mix with water, milk, or soy milk for a spicy, mildly sweet drink. Regular and decaf food-service sizes available.

CHAI LATTE TEA (DBA CAPPUCCINE, INC.)

1285 Valdivia Way
Palm Springs, CA 92262
(800) 511-3127
Fax: (760) 864-7360
Web site: www.cappuccine.com
e-mail: cappuccine@worldnet.att.net
Mixes can be blended with ice or in a granita/slush or cappuccino machine. Add water or water and ice to serve hot or cold. Nicely balanced blend of black tea and Indian spices. Available in resealable containers and bags at specialty food markets, tea and coffee shops, and restaurants.

CHOICE ORGANIC TEA (DBA GRANUM, INC.)

2901 Northeast Blakeley Street
Seattle, WA 98105
(206) 525-0051
Fax: (206) 523-9750
Every ingredient, from the teas to the spices, is certified organic in three offerings: Herbal Blend with cardamom, chamomile, ginger, fennel, peppermint, licorice, cloves, and black pepper; Chai and Decaf Chai, each with organic black teas and spices. Available in natural food stores in ready-to-brew twenty-serving boxes. Wholesale and mail orders accepted.

DAVID RIO COFFEE & TEA: SEE TAJ MAHAL CHAI

DAVIDSON'S, INC.

Box 11214
Reno, NV 89510
(800) 882-5888
Fax: (775) 356-3713
e-mail: tea@davidson.reno.nv.us
Three chai selections in charming packages of eight sachets each: Classic Chai made with a blend of Indian and Chinese black teas and chai spices; and two herbal selections, Herbal Chai and Mandarin Chai with Anise, made with blackberry, chamomile, and spices. Wholesale orders of loose-leaf Classic and Herbal Chais accepted.

EASTERN CHAI

23 Emmons Street
Long Branch, NJ 07740
(732) 571-9005
Fax: (732) 571-8095
Web site: www.danroc.com
e-mail: easternchai@danroc.com
Premixed powdered chai mix to which you add water, and voilà — chai! Available in food service and consumer sizes.

GAIA CHAI

PO Box 110327
Anchorage, AK 99508
(907) 276-4242
Fax: (907) 345-7214
Web site: www.gaiachai.com
e-mail: specialteas@gaiachai.com
One-quart consumer-sized and food service-sized chais in aseptic package of concentrates, made with whole-leaf estate teas from Darjeeling, Nilgiri, Ceylon, and Assam. Original Spiced Chai and Chocolate Chai, plus a loose chai mix to brew at home. Sold in natural food stores and upscale markets.

GOLDEN AGE TEA COMPANY: SEE SOJOURNS, NEW ADVENTURES IN TEA

GOLDEN MOON

PO Box 1646
Woodinville, WA 98072
(425) 576-0179
Fax: (425) 576-0410
Web site: www.goldenmoontea.com
Exceptionally fine Darjeeling tea makes this loose-leaf chai and spice mixture an elegant, delicious drink. Has just the right amount of fine spices including whole green cardamom pods, cinnamon, and cloves. Lovely! Packaged in 5-ounce bags, available at upscale markets.

GRANELLI BOLD SPICED DELHI CHAI (DBA GRANELLI ICE)

22122 20th Avenue SE, Suite 159
Bothell, WA 98021-4407
(800) 472-6482 or (425) 487-6824
Fax: (425) 487-6826
e-mail: granelliice@integrityol.com
Granelli Bold Spiced Delhi Chai is a liquid concentrate blend of exotic spices and black teas without preservatives. Available in shelf-stable bottles of 6.35 ounces or food service sizes.

GRANUM, INC.: SEE CHOICE ORGANIC TEA

HARNEY & SONS

11 East Main Street
Village Green PO Box 676
Salisbury, CT 06068
(888) Harney-T
Fax: (860) 435-5044

The Indian Spice Tea mixture is ideal for those who like to experiment and create their own authentic chais. Add boiling water and serve as a spicy plain tea, or add milk, sugar, and additional spices as desired for a chai latte.

HIMALAYAN HIGHLAND TEA CO.

1702 South Highway 121, Suite 607-189
Lewisville, TX 75067
(800) 580-8585 or (972) 436-1590
Fax: (972) 221-6770
e-mail: bduarte@flash.net

Rough-cut tea and hearty spices of anise, pepper, coriander, cloves, cardamom, and cinnamon infuse this loose-leaf masala chai packaged in small wooden boxes. This is the "real McCoy" masala chai as it is drunk in Nepal.

HONEST TEA™

4905 Del Ray Avenue, Suite 304
Bethesda, MD 20814
(301) 652-3556
Fax: (301) 652-3557
Web site: www.honesttea.com

Kashmiri chai in a bottle made with all-natural ingredients and freshly brewed Indian black tea with spring water and crushed cardamom, cinnamon, orange peel, cloves, pepper, ginger, and sugar cane juice. Open up and enjoy. Available in 16-ounce jars with vacuum twist caps.

LEAVES PURE LEAVES

1392 Lowrie Avenue
South San Francisco, CA 94080
(650) 583-1157

This delightful tea and herbal infusion company has created an Herbs & Spice tea bag that's perfect for the herbal chai lover. Enjoy an infusion of licorice root, cinnamon, cloves, orange peel, rose hips, lemon verbena, and rosebuds. Exquisite. Available in fine shops and food stores throughout the country.

MASALA CHAI COMPANY

PO Box 8375
Santa Cruz, CA 95061
(831) 475-8881 or (718) 486-0024

Since 1980, this pioneer chai manufacturer has developed a variety of addictive chais including a traditional Masala Chai or Decaf Masala Chai, plus male and female energy tonics called AphroTEAsiac, St.-John's-wort/Ginkgo with Darjeeling, Taoist Elixir Chai with Green Tea, Reishi Mushroom, and Siberian Ginseng. Other choices include instant chai mixes, tea bags, gallon bottles, and food-service quantities.

THE METROPOLITAN TEA COMPANY

1010 Niagara Street
Buffalo, NY 14213
(800) 388-0351
Fax: (800) 319-8327 or (416) 588-7040
Web site: www.metrotea.com
e-mail: sales@metrotea.com
Available as loose-leaf teas and tea bags are Mocha Chai and Spice Chai, a masala-style blend sold wholesale to specialty food markets, coffee and tea shops, and restaurants.

MOCAFE: SEE PRECIOUS DIVINITY CHAI

MOUNTAIN CHAI (DBA CELESTIAL SEASONINGS)

4600 Sleepytime Drive
Boulder, CO 80301-3292
(303) 530-5300
Assam black and Chinese green teas are part of the recipe for six different flavors: Authentic, Decaf Authentic, Sweetened, Decaf Sweetened, Mocha, and Green Tea. Sold in liquid concentrates at regional supermarkets, specialty food stores, and natural food stores in 32-ounce (1-quart) and 128-ounce (1-gallon) containers for food-service clients. More flavors coming soon.

MY CHAI

225 West Flores
Tucson, AZ 85705
(877) 692-4248 or (520) 628-9811
Fax: (520) 628-9807
This Indian-owned chai company offers exceptional Assam teas blended with fresh spices to be brewed on the stove top or in the microwave, adding the milk and sweetener of your choice. Unbleached tea bags are just part of a company-wide policy of recycling paper and using natural packaging. Available in Original Chai and Decaffeinated Chai, with twenty-five tea bags per package. Commercial bulk quantities available for food service.

NEW DELHI RESTAURANT

160 Ellis Street
San Francisco, CA 94102
(415) 387-8470
Fax: (415) 387-1024
This classic Indian restaurant serves an authentic masala chai tea you can enjoy with its menu; you can also buy packages of premeasured, preblended masala chai made with a combination of Assam and Darjeeling teas and spices. Each half-ounce packet makes four cups. Open daily except Sunday; mail order accepted.

NUB CIRCUS

1723 Soquel Avenue
Santa Cruz, CA 95062
(888) Nub-Chai (682-2424)
Web site: www.nub.com
e-mail: Elixir@nubchai.com
What do a group of "random performers" do for fun? They pitch a 1,000-foot Bedouin tent, sing, dance, and tell stories (always with a strong point, or "nub"). To refresh the audience, they sell 100 percent certifiably organic chai made with loose-leaf Ceylon teas and exotic herbs and spice mixtures, or caffeine-free with herbs alone for a spicy infusion. Add milk and/or sweetener, if you prefer.

OREGON CHAI, INC.

725 Southeast Ninth Avenue, Suite T
Portland, OR 97214
(888) 874-2424 or (503) 234-1430
Fax: (503) 234-1386
Web site: www.oregonchai.com
e-mail: nirvana@oregonchai.com/wholesale
Four chai products are offered in ready-to-mix liquid concentrates sold in "Bag-in-Box" in 1½-gallon, 12-ounce, or 32-ounce sizes at specialty food markets, tea shops, and restaurants. Flavors are Original Chai Tea Latte, Kashmir Green Tea, Chai Charger, Organic Chai, and caffeine-free Herbal Bliss with chamomile.

PACIFIC CHAI

6216-D Seabrook Road
Lanham-Seabrook, MD 20706
(888) 882-4248 or (301) 429-9440
Fax: (301) 429-9442
Web site: www.pacificchai.com
e-mail: sales@pacificchai.com
Nicely balanced chai mix suitable for a granita, or for iced or hot chai lattes. The black and Darjeeling teas and spices are in a powdered form with a handy measuring spoon; simply mix with water. Available in a single-serving pouch, 1-pound bag, or 6-pound jar. Order from the toll-free number or online.

PRECIOUS DIVINITY CHAI (DBA MOCAFE)

PO Box 6373
Laguna Niguel, CA 92607
(949) 831-8656 or (888) 662-2334
Fax: (949) 831-2390
Web site: www.4mocafe.com
e-mail: mocafe@sprynet.com
Rich, complex flavor profile with black teas offered in half-gallon liquid concentrates at fine grocers and food-service venues. An award winner!

REPUBLIC OF TEA

8 Digital Drive, #100
Novato, CA 94949
(415) 382-3400
Web site under construction
e-mail: Barbara@Republicoftea.com
A full line of chais, including liquid concentrates, in 10-ounce bottles: Decaf Chai Latte Tea of Awareness, Maté Latte Chai All Night Samba Herb Tea, Chai of Many Virtues Journey of Health Tea, and Republic Chai Traveler's Tea. Full-leaf versions of Republic Chai and Republic Green Chai of Many Virtues are sold in 3½-ounce round tins. The teas used are black Assams and Darjeelings or various green teas; herbals include maté. Other choices include Loose Leaf Chai of Many Virtues with Herbs, and Cardamom Cinnamon Warm the Heart Herb Tea, an herbal blend. Sold at fine grocery stores everywhere.

SATTWA CHAI

Box 805
Newberg, OR 97132
(503) 538-4715
Fax: (503) 538-5125
Since 1994 Sattwa Chai has microbrewed Taj Assam black tea for Sattwa Sun, a mix of black tea and spices; Kovalam Spice Chai, a spicier chai; Shanti Herbal Chai, a caffeine-free dry blend of chamomile and herbs; Choco Chai, a spiced cocoa mix with spices, but no tea; a spicy peppermint chai concentrate; Sattwa Herbal Chai Concentrate; and a traditional black-tea-and-spice concentrate. Concentrates come in 32-ounce packages, powders in packages of 2.1 to 3.25 ounces. Available at all fine upscale markets. Sattwa means "cosmic force of equilibrium" or "normal balanced state of a healthy mind."

SEATTLE CHAI (DBA BLUE WILLOW TEA COMPANY)

911 East Pike Street, #204
Seattle, WA 98122
(206) 325-9889
Fax: (206) 325-7153
e-mail: fjm@bluewillowtea.com
A dry mix available in 4-ounce packages or in bulk quantities made with 50 percent high-quality Nilgiri tea from southern India and 50 percent freshly ground spices. Designed to be brewed with water on the stove top; add soy milk or regular milk plus any sweetener you desire. Distributed primarily in natural food stores or by mail order. Wholesale orders accepted.

SOJOURNS, NEW ADVENTURES IN TEA (DBA GOLDEN AGE TEA COMPANY)

48900 Milmont Drive
Fremont, CA 94538
(800) 300-5212
Fax: (510) 656-0590
Web site: www.goldenagetea.com
The Casablanca Spice blend — made up of China black tea, cardamom, cinnamon, and ginger — makes a delightful base for chai. Available in 1.27-ounce packages of 18 tea bags each.

STARBUCKS

Locations everywhere.
The sprawling coffee "pub" of the United States with more than 1500 stores offers TAZO chai, along with many other tea selections from its newest partner.

STASH TEA

Box 910
Portland, OR 97207
(503) 684-4482
Fax: (503) 684-4482
Web site: www.stashtea.com
e-mail: stash@stashtea.com
A Green Chai and a Chai Spice Tea, made from Assam and Nilgiri teas, are sold either loose leaf or in tea bags at major supermarkets and specialty food shops, by mail order, and online. Food-service bulk quantities available.

TAJ MAHAL CHAI (DBA DAVID RIO COFFEE & TEA)

4104 24th Street, #592
San Francisco, CA 94114
(415) 642-1066
Fax: (415) 642-1067
Web site: www.davidrio.com
e-mail: chai@davidrio.com or
davidrio@sirius.com
Taj Mahal Elephant Vanilla, Tiger Spice, and Tortoise Green Tea are the three easy-to-use powdered mixes available in 1-, 14-, and 25-pound sizes for both retail and food-service use. Order online or by mail order.

TAYLOR MAID FARMS

6793 McKinley Street
Sebastopol, CA 95472
(707) 824-9110
Web site: www.taylormaidfarms.com
An authentic, highly aromatic loose-leaf organic Indian tea blended with natural spices. Sold in 1.5- and 3-ounce tins that make 18 and 36 cups of chai, respectively. Offers an entire line of organic black and green teas and tisanes.

TAZO

Box 66
Portland, OR 97207
(800) 299-9445
Fax: (503) 231-8801
Web site: www.tazo.com (under construction)
Organic Tazo Chai is available in liquid concentrate and in a loose-leaf version with a combination of fresh spices and teas. Available by direct mail and in fine food shops nationwide, and soon at its new parent company, Starbucks.

TEAISM CHAI (DBA TEAISM — A TEA HOUSE)

2009 R Street Northwest
Washington, DC 20024
(888) 8-Teaism or (202) 667-3827
Fax: (202) 667-3286
Second location opening in downtown
D.C. soon.
An authentic chai blend, Spice Mix can be made plain or with sweetener and/or milk. Sold in-house, or by mail order in 4-ounce sizes; wholesale orders accepted.

TEAROOM T

Qi Botanical Tea, Ltd.
2460 Heather Street
Vancouver, BC V5Z 3H9
(604) 874-8320 or (888) 291-Teas
Web site: www.tealeaves.com
Divinitea Chai — Chaipuccino black tea chai is a smooth and very spicy chai. Each tea bag makes 1 quart of concentrated chai, which can be refrigerated for up to one week. Other flavors are Heaven & Earth Herbal Spiced Chai and Maharajah's Mocha Chai. Dee-lish!

THIRD STREET CHAI

3200 Valmont
Boulder, CO 80201
(303) 442-5117
Fax: (303) 442-5742
Web site: www.3rdstreetchai.com
e-mail: john@3rdstreetchai.com
Expedition 1: Spiced Tea of India in original, decaf, and organic Darjeeling is available at natural food stores, specialty food stores, restaurants, and tea shops. One- and 2-quart sizes and 1-gallon sizes in concentrate are sold. Bulk spice mixture available.

UP N' ATOM

5243 Highway 9
Felton, CA 95018
(408) 335-1767
Web site: www.upnatom.com
e-mail: Omirag@cruzio.com
Long-leaf Chinese black teas are blended with imported chopped spices for Chai and Caffeine-Free Chai, to use with or without milk and sweetener. Available at specialty and natural food stores and tea shops or online. Wholesale orders accepted.

XANADU EXOTIC CHAI

2181 Northwest Nicolai Street
Portland, OR 97210
(503) 227-4490
Fax: (503) 225-9604
e-mail: products@coffeebeanintl.com
Tins of loose-leaf or bagged tea are offered in specialty food markets, tea and coffee shops, and restaurants. The nicely balanced mélange blends savory spices and Indian Assam tea with amethyst sugar crystals for a light, sweet taste. Wholesale orders accepted.

ZEN CHAI

PO Box 3031
Homer, AK 99603
Phone and fax: (907) 235-2100
Web site: www.xyz.net/~zen/
e-mail: zen@xyz.net
Freshly ground spices make the difference in this liquid concentrate made with clear Alaska water, loose-leaf black teas, sugar, and just the right balance of cardamom, cinnamon, and ginger. Add milk, heat it up, and enjoy.

publications

TEA TALK: A NEWSLETTER ON THE PLEASURES OF TEA

PO Box 860
Sausalito, CA 94966
(415) 331-1557
Diana Rosen's publication on tea. $17.95 for four issues.

the tea gardens of india

Darjeeling

The following are the tea gardens currently operating in Darjeeling. Most major tea vendors offer these gardens' produce. Remember that the plucking, season, and type of processing (into green, oolong, or black tea) determine how the finest Darjeelings taste in the cup. The list also includes smaller tea gardens that have not yet achieved the vigor and stability of the classic ones, but do offer a taste adventure. Generally, single-estate Darjeelings are more expensive than blends, although each category can offer a satisfying cup. For more information ask your tea vendor to tell you more about this year's crop and its flavor profiles; they do vary slightly from year to year. The gardens are:

Aloobari
Ambootia
Arya
Avongrove
Balasun
Bandamtam
Banockburn
Castleton
Chamong
Chongtong (Sirisi) Dhajea
Dilaram
Dooteriah
Gidhapahar
Gielle
Ging
Glenburn

Goomtee (includes Mohan Majhua and Narbada Majhua)
Gopaldhara
Gyabaree/Millikthong
Happy Valley
Jogmaya
Jungpana
Kalej Valley
Lingia
Liza Hill
Longview
Lopchu
Mahalderm
Makaibari
Margaret's Hope
Marybong
Mim
Mission Hill
Monteviot/Edenvale
Moondakotee
Mullootar
Nagri
Nagri Farm
Namring Tea Estate
North Tukvar
Oaks
Okayti
Orange Valley
Pandam
Pashok
Phoobsering
Phoobong
Phuguri
Pussimbing
Rangaroon
Ringtong
Risheehat
Rohini
Runglee Rungliot
Rungmook Cedars
Rungneet

Samabeong
Seeyok
Selim Hill
Selimbong
Sepoydhura (Chamling)
Singbulli
Singell
Singtom
Snowview
Soom
Soureni
Spring Side
Steinthal
Sungma
Teesta Valley (an area and an estate)
Thurbo
Tindharia
Tukdah
Tukvar
Tumsong
Vah Tukvar

Khongea
Koilamari
Mangalam
Manjushree
Meleng
Nahorhabi
Numalighur
Rupai
Sangsua
Satyanarian
Seajuli
Sesson
Sonarie
Sufflaghur
Tara
Thowra
Toonabarrie
Towkok

Assam

Garden names to look for in Assam teas are:
Behora
Bogapani
Borpatra
Deamoolie
Dejoo
Ethelwold
Guilliahary
Halmari
Harmutty
Jay Shree

Nilgiri

Garden names of high-end Nilgiri estates include:
Burnside
Craigmore (Pascoes Woodlands Gardens)
Grahamsland
Korakundha
Oothu
Tiger Hill

index

Note: Page numbers in *italics* indicate photographs.

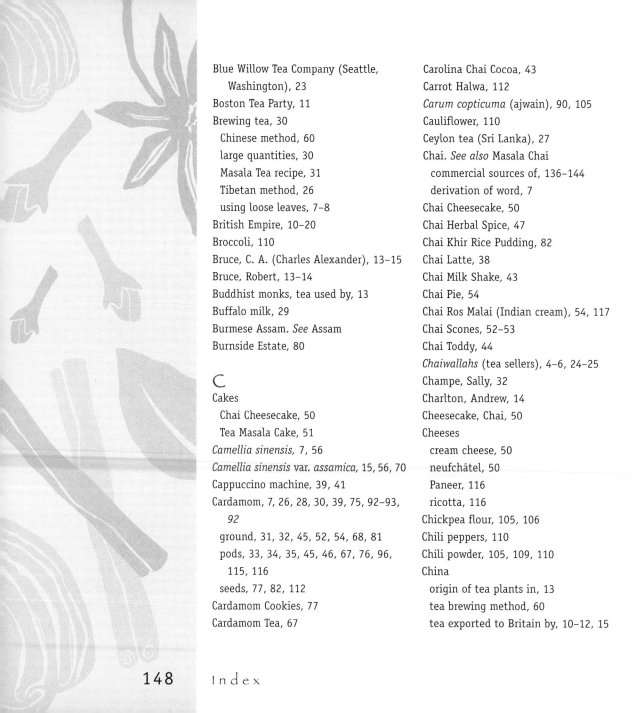

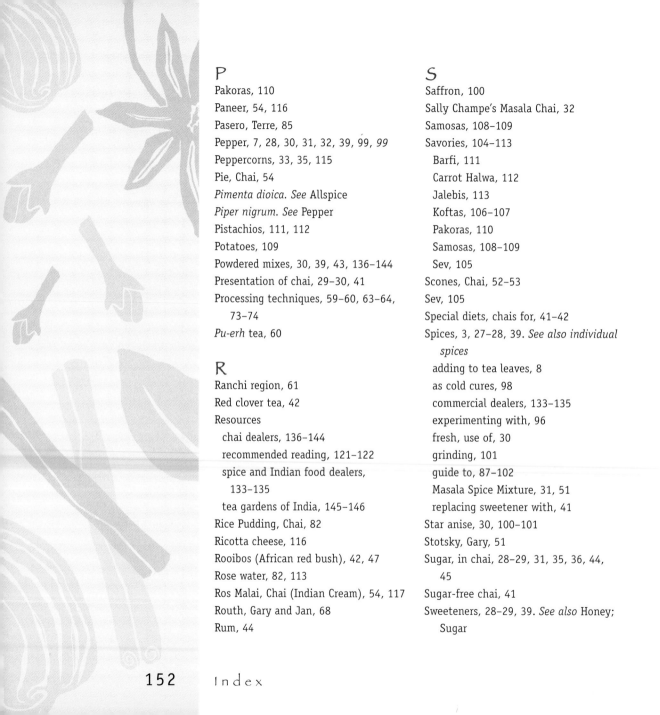

other storey titles you will enjoy

The Book of Green Tea, by Diana Rosen. A comprehensive guide to the history, varieties, and health benefits of this traditional and enjoyable Asian beverage. Includes recipes for food and beauty and health care products. 160 pages. Paperback. ISBN 1-58017-090-0.

Country Tea Parties, by Maggie Stuckey. Organized by month, this book offers interesting, creative ideas for twelve special tea parties. Beautiful four-color illustrations by Carolyn Bucha highlight the menus and recipes. 64 pages. Hardcover. ISBN 0-88266-935-4.

Herbal Teas, by Kathleen Brown. This guide to blending and brewing healthful herb teas includes easy-to-make recipes and anecdotes from several renowned herbalists. Readers will find teas for the head and throat, digestion, nervous system, lungs, bones and joints, back, male and female reproductive systems, circulatory system, and skin. 160 pages. Paperback. ISBN 1-58017-099-4.

Keeping Entertaining Simple, by Martha Storey. This fun-to-read tips book offers hundreds of ideas for low-fuss, low-anxiety entertaining with friends, for the holidays, and for business purposes. 160 pages. Paperback. ISBN 1-58017-056-0.

Steeped in Tea, by Diana Rosen. Using a room-by-room approach, this book explores both the drinking and nondrinking uses for tea, including decorating and crafting with tea, making tea health and beauty products and gifts, and creating special places to truly savor the tea-taking experience. Suggestions for traditional tea events and theme tea gardens are also included. 180 pages. Paperback. ISBN 1-58017-093-5.

Tea with Friends, by Elizabeth Knight. A year's worth of occasions to bring friends together around a pot of tea. Each party contains suggested menus and activities, and includes elegant watercolor paintings by noted Caspari artist Carolyn Bucha. 64 pages. Hardcover. ISBN 1-58017-050-1.

These books and other Storey Books are available at your bookstore, farm store, garden center, or directly from Storey Books, Schoolhouse Road, Pownal, Vermont 05261, or by calling 1-800-441-5700. Or visit our Web site at www.storey.com.